T0321461

Concept Parsing Algorithms (CPA) for Textual Analysis and Discovery:

Emerging Research and Opportunities

Uri Shafrir
University of Toronto, Canada

Masha Etkind
Ryerson University, Canada

A volume in the Advances in
Computational Intelligence and
Robotics (ACIR) Book Series

Published in the United States of America by
    IGI Global
    Information Science Reference (an imprint of IGI Global)
    701 E. Chocolate Avenue
    Hershey PA, USA 17033
    Tel: 717-533-8845
    Fax: 717-533-8661
    E-mail: cust@igi-global.com
    Web site: http://www.igi-global.com

Library of Congress Cataloging-in-Publication Data

Names: Shafrir, Uri, author. | Etkind, Masha, 1946- author.
Title: Concept parsing algorithms (CPA) for textual analysis and discovery :
  emerging research and opportunities / by Uri Shafrir and Masha Etkind.
Description: Hershey, PA : Information Science Reference, [2017]
Identifiers: LCCN 2016056028| ISBN 9781522521761 (hardcover) | ISBN
  9781522521778 (ebook)
Subjects: LCSH: Text processing (Computer science) | Electronic information
  resource searching. | Sublanguage. | Semantics--Methodology.
Classification: LCC QA76.9.T48 S46 2017 | DDC 401/.40285--dc23 LC record available at https://
lccn.loc.gov/2016056028

This book is published in the IGI Global book series Advances in Computational Intelligence and Robotics (ACIR) (ISSN: 2327-0411; eISSN: 2327-042X)

British Cataloguing in Publication Data
A Cataloguing in Publication record for this book is available from the British Library.

For electronic access to this publication, please contact: eresources@igi-global.com.

Advances in Computational Intelligence and Robotics (ACIR) Book Series

ISSN:2327-0411
EISSN:2327-042X

Editor-in-Chief: Ivan Giannoccaro, University of Salento, Italy

MISSION

While intelligence is traditionally a term applied to humans and human cognition, technology has progressed in such a way to allow for the development of intelligent systems able to simulate many human traits. With this new era of simulated and artificial intelligence, much research is needed in order to continue to advance the field and also to evaluate the ethical and societal concerns of the existence of artificial life and machine learning.

The **Advances in Computational Intelligence and Robotics (ACIR) Book Series** encourages scholarly discourse on all topics pertaining to evolutionary computing, artificial life, computational intelligence, machine learning, and robotics. ACIR presents the latest research being conducted on diverse topics in intelligence technologies with the goal of advancing knowledge and applications in this rapidly evolving field.

COVERAGE

- Artificial Life
- Algorithmic Learning
- Automated Reasoning
- Adaptive and Complex Systems
- Computational Logic
- Intelligent control
- Heuristics
- Fuzzy Systems
- Brain Simulation
- Cognitive Informatics

IGI Global is currently accepting manuscripts for publication within this series. To submit a proposal for a volume in this series, please contact our Acquisition Editors at Acquisitions@igi-global.com or visit: http://www.igi-global.com/publish/.

Titles in this Series

For a list of additional titles in this series, please visit:
http://www.igi-global.com/book-series/advances-computational-intelligence-robotics/73674

Handbook of Research on Machine Learning Innovations and Trends
Aboul Ella Hassanien (Cairo University, Egypt) and Tarek Gaber (Suez Canal University, Egypt)
Information Science Reference • ©2017 • 1093pp • H/C (ISBN: 9781522522294) • US $465.00

Handbook of Research on Soft Computing and Nature-Inspired Algorithms
Shishir K. Shandilya (Bansal Institute of Research and Technology, India) Smita Shandilya
(Sagar Institute of Research Technology and Science, India) Kusum Deep (Indian Institute
of Technology Roorkee, India) and Atulya K. Nagar (Liverpool Hope University, UK)
Information Science Reference • ©2017 • 627pp • H/C (ISBN: 9781522521280) • US $280.00

Membrane Computing for Distributed Control of Robotic Swarms Emerging Research...
Andrei George Florea (Politehnica University of Bucharest, Romania) and Cătălin Buiu
(Politehnica University of Bucharest, Romania)
Information Science Reference • ©2017 • 119pp • H/C (ISBN: 9781522522805) • US $160.00

Recent Developments in Intelligent Nature-Inspired Computing
Srikanta Patnaik (SOA University, India)
Information Science Reference • ©2017 • 264pp • H/C (ISBN: 9781522523222) • US $185.00

Ubiquitous Machine Learning and Its Applications
Pradeep Kumar (Maulana Azad National Urdu University, India) and Arvind Tiwari (DIT
University, India)
Information Science Reference • ©2017 • 258pp • H/C (ISBN: 9781522525455) • US $185.00

Advanced Image Processing Techniques and Applications
N. Suresh Kumar (VIT University, India) Arun Kumar Sangaiah (VIT University, India) M.
Arun (VIT University, India) and S. Anand (VIT University, India)
Information Science Reference • ©2017 • 439pp • H/C (ISBN: 9781522520535) • US $290.00

For an enitre list of titles in this series, please visit:
http://www.igi-global.com/book-series/advances-computational-intelligence-robotics/73674

701 East Chocolate Avenue, Hershey, PA 17033, USA
Tel: 717-533-8845 x100 • Fax: 717-533-8661
E-Mail: cust@igi-global.com • www.igi-global.com

Table of Contents

Chapter 8

Preface

The new reality of digital libraries raise the specter of a digital library containing all of humanity's communicative artifacts, and the obvious questions: Are there substantial benefits for learning, research and other scholarly activities from such novel reality? And if so, what new tools and research methodologies may help to unlock such benefits?

In this book focus on those parts of a universal digital library containing documents that communicate knowledge with controlled vocabularies of sublanguages, mostly in the various STEM disciplines, e.g., Science; Technology; Engineering; and Mathematics.

Unlike in natural language where a word often has many connotations, in controlled vocabulary of a sublanguage a unique 'code word' acts like proper name of a concept, whose meaning is encoded in its building blocks, namely, co-occurring sub-ordinate concepts and relations. We are particularly interested in tools and methodologies that allow researchers and learners to explore and discover content 'code words', as well as to index the conceptual content of documents.

In the following eight chapters, we describe *Concept Parsing Algorithms (CPA)*, a novel methodology of discovering building blocks of a concept. As well as two applications: *Meaning Equivalence Reusable Learning Objects (MERLO)* and *Interactive Concept Discovery (InCoD)*. MERLO is a digital interactive assessment tool for depth of understanding of content in any knowledge domain. InCoD is semantic search tool for controlled vocabularies in sublanguages, with Lexical Labels of concepts and their building blocks, that encode the conceptual content of documents in contexts in disciplines in different knowledge domains. It is also applicable to an individual organization's digital data base with the particular organization's own controlled vocabulary. We report on what we have learned from evaluative implementations over the last decade of the novel Pedagogy for Conceptual Thinking that focus learners' attention on conceptual content and enhance learning outcomes (Shafrir & Etkind, 2006; Etkind, Kenett & Shafrir, 2016; Shafrir & Kenett, 2016).

Acknowledgment

This book evolved as conclusion of many discussions over the last 15 years with our colleagues and dear friends Vyacheslav V. Ivanov, the late Victor Erlich, and the late Irving E. Sigel, that are the foundation of the research described in this book. We thank Ivanov and Erlich for generously sharing their deep knowledge of semiotics and its application to conceptual context of controlled vocabularies. We thank Sigel for generously sharing his knowledge and ideas of representational competence as a mediator of meaning, and context for the development of meaning equivalence.

Chapter 1

Representation of Meaning in Different Semiotic Systems

ABSTRACT

This chapter describe issues related to the ability to represent meaning in different semiotic systems that plays a major role in the development of infants and continues to influence humans throughout life. The semiosphere is the symbolic environment into which a child grows, that defines the types of representations encoded in the developing child's mind. It is dynamic and multifunctional, and includes a class of meaning-preserving transformations. These symbolic transformations generate multiple representations with equivalent meaning, and inevitably result in the over-determination of meaning within the semiosphere. Early meaning, derived from perceptual cues, evolve to mature meaning derived from combinations of perceptual cues and memories of their consequences. Adults generate intentional responses to meaning of combinations of perceptual and intellectual stimuli, and are aware of representation of meaning in different semiotic systems.

INTRODUCTION

The cognitive and neuroscience revolutions at the end of the 20th century have advanced the efforts of identifying and localizing cognitive processes. One of the enduring problems in cognitive psychology has been that of representation in its many forms, the activities of representing, the uses of

DOI: 10.4018/978-1-5225-2176-1.ch001

representations in learning, memory, and thinking; and the mechanisms that control the formation of representations (Cocking, 2012).

A third revolution in technology is now expanding cognitive and neuroscience research in new directions and the databases are once again growing. Imaging technologies are enabling researchers to test theoretical conceptions of cognitive representation more precisely. At the same time, new learning technologies, especially computer and interactive technologies, are expanding the scope by adding new issues of representation, such as visual cognition.

'While current evidence suggests that incremental learning models show promise for addressing the acquisition of perceptual and conceptual knowledge structure in the brain, other possibilities remain that posit more dedicated functions to occipital and temporal cortex, with unsupervised learning applying throughout the visual system in a more feed-forward manner that relies on biases in low-level image statistics between stimulus categories to explain any category preferences in occipitotemporal cortex... On this view, most of the flexibility and adaptability of knowledge representation is handled by the prefrontal cortex... Indeed, it is interesting to note that conceptual "broadening" is observed when the task is categorization... as well as when the task requires individuation' (Gotts et al., 2014). This leads Gotts (2016) to suggest that it is 'raising the possibility that prefrontal cortex has a more general role in automatically extracting more abstract category-like structure from individual objects presented in the same context. At a minimum, the future experiments... will help to delineate the bounds on existing incremental learning proposals, allowing us to see how much of the adult knowledge organization is plausibly based in supervised versus unsupervised learning mechanisms, as well as to what extent innate anatomical constraints might contribute'.

Indeed, because of new evidence and new methodologies, the long-standing research topic of representational thinking has moved from speculation to science. In this evolution, the science of representation has played an important role as a unifying concept across many research disciplines.

During the last century increasing efforts were made to understand mental functioning, such as thought and language. The interest and proliferation of research in cognitive science lead to an exponential increase in approaches to the study of the development of representational thought and language. Cognitive science evolved into an interdisciplinary science. Central to this science was the development of the theory of representation (Sigel, 2012).

The particular choice of content may lead an investigator to findings that are relative and relevant to that particular knowledge domain. Do findings from a particular study (e.g., representational understanding of mathematics) allow for universal generalization to other knowledge domains? The essential meaning that undergirds the various uses of representation from an essential perspective, irrespective of context or content, is that a representation stands for something other than itself: its identity is relative to its referent; it is not an independent entity.

Yet, in the psychological literature, the term representation is often used without providing any context. Thus in psychological parlance, invoking the term representation alone does not provide a common referent, thereby leading to misunderstanding and miscommunication. It seems that the meaning is dependent on the epistemological orientation of the user. If the reader of the text employing a particular term does not share the epistemological base or the referents for the term, it then results in misunderstanding. These representations are all mental, but it is important to realize that the same representation may have a common referent but a different meaning. The meaning is in the head of the speaker and a different meaning may be in the head of the listener.

The way that knowledge is acquired, organized, and made available for use require the individual to transform everyday perceptual and sensory experiences into some form of mental representation. This mental activity is a necessary requirement for adapting and functioning effectively in complex and diverse environments. In this chapter, the focus is on applicability of representation of concepts, generally accepted as basic to knowledge acquisition, organization, and application (Sigel, 2012).

The term representation refers to an instance that is equivalent to its referent; for example, the word landscape is equivalent to the three-dimensional natural landscape. Simply put, the word landscape has a meaning similar to not only the natural landscape, but also to a painting or a photograph of a landscape. In fact, each of these three instances (the word, the painting, and the photograph) are equivalent, but not identical. What makes the three instances equivalent is the common meaning attributed to them.

Representation refers to instances that are equivalent in meaning, but different in mode of expression. Although there is general agreement among most behavioral scientists, philosophers, and educators as to the basic definition, there is disagreement as to the universality, the origins, the developmental course, and the practical use of the term representation. The reasons for such diversity may be due to the specific aspects of representation under study.

Bever (1986) summarized the issues where he wrote: 'There are two fundamental processes that occur when we perceive and represent the world. We automatically form representations of what we perceive. We integrate conflicts in those representations by accessing perceptual and conceptual knowledge of a variety of kinds. The integration of such representational conflicts is itself accompanied by a release of emotional energy. These processes are functional in everyday perception, conceptual development, and problem solving.' (pp. 325-326)

The concept 'representation' has been at the center of psychology, neurobiology and artificial intelligence for the last several decades. The ability to represent experience has been viewed by psychologists as a prerequisite for development (Sigel, 1970; Vygotsky, 1978). They also believe that changes in the nature of mental representations lie at the core of cognitive abilities. Definitions of representation may vary, but most share a common view of representation as the ability to create and to maintain an internal trace - a representation - of experience. The age at which the newborn infant unequivocally demonstrates the ability to represent experience has been revised downward continuously. For example, it has been shown that infants as young as 6 weeks old can generate actions on the basis of stored representations (Meltzoff & Moore, 1994).

The concept of representation also plays a fundamental role in disciplines other than psychology that are concerned with development, such as neurobiology and artificial intelligence. Dudai (1989), working within a neurobiological developmental perspective, defined internal representation as 'neuronally encoded structured versions of the world which could potentially guide behaviour' (p. 5); Dudai also defined learning as experience-driven generation of new or lasting changes to existing internal representations. Artificial intelligence researchers, who use computer models to simulate development, are divided on the role of representation in development and learning. Connectionists view development as synonymous with nonrepresentational learning through parallel distributed processing (PDP), that is, parallel interactions of weighted excitatory and inhibitory connections among large numbers of neurons (McLelland, 1995). According to this view development is an implicit, experience-driven process, that build gradually on existing knowledge (e.g., patterns of activation weights), and does not lend itself to easy mapping on explicit representations and propositional knowledge.

Children's knowledge about representations is initially acquired at an early age; young children come to realize that culturally defined signs (e.g., names, numbers, pictures, maps) have 'dual lives': In addition to being objects in their own right, they also represent - stand for - other objects, events, or ideas (De-Loache, 1993). Children learn early that other ordinary and familiar items may also have dual lives, for example, a hat and a scarf may be familiar playthings on their own. However, when the infant is being dressed in these objects, they represent - create an expectation of - an impending stroll outdoors. Charles Darwin described his own observation of such an event where an engraving may be a familiar object on its own but at age 3 years a child recognizes it as the image of his grandfather 'whom he had not seen for exactly six months, instantly recognized him and mentioned a whole string of events which had occurred whilst visiting him, and which had certainly never been mentioned in the interval' (Darwin, 1877; p. 291).

As children develop, they become more knowledgeable about the relationships between signs and referents, signifying and signified. They come to realize that the mapping of signs on referents is not a simple, one-to-one relationship, and that a specific sign stands not only for a specific object, but for a category of objects. For example, the utterance 'dog' may initially refer only to the family dog; however, later exposure to other dogs will eventually convert 'dog' into a category label. As children develop, they also come to realize that a referent may be signified by different signs in a sign system; for example, 'daddy' is equivalent to 'father', who also has a proper name. Also that a referent may be signified by signs belonging to different sign systems, e.g., a color photograph, a video clip, and the utterance 'dog' all refer to the same beloved family pet.

What are the mediators of the development of children's knowledge about the relationships between signs and referents? Studies conducted by Sigel and his collaborators (e.g., Sigel, Anderson, & Shapiro, 1966; Sigel & McBane, 1967; Sigel & Olmstead, 1970a, 1970b) showed that low socioeconomic status (SES) children, in contrast to middle-class children, had difficulties in classifying certain two-dimensional representations - pictures - but not three-dimensional models of the same objects. Sigel and his collaborators hypothesized that the ability to master and to operate effectively on this many-to-many correspondences between signs and referents lies at the core of development, and defined it as the conservation of meaning, or representational competence. Following these initial findings, Sigel and his collaborators have conducted programmatic research on the development of representational competence in children of different ages, as well as different

SES and parenting styles (Sigel, 1970; 1986; Sigel & Cocking, 1977). They concluded that the acquisition of representational competence is related to distancing acts, which they defined as behaviors of parents, caregivers, and teachers that help the child to separate perceptually accessible features of the here-and-now from their distal, intellective representations, thus facilitating the development of representational competence.

MAIN FOCUS OF THE CHAPTER

Issues, Controversies, Problems

Our goal in this chapter is to examine different aspects of the construct 'representational competence'. We begin by examining some aspects of the ability to use different sign systems, and proceed by formulating a definition of representational competence that lends itself to empirical refutation (Shafrir, 2012).

Eco (1976) defined a sign as 'everything that, on the grounds of a previously established social convention, can be taken as *something standing for something else*' (italics in original; p. 16). A sign system is a collection of one or more types of signs, together with a set of rules that specify how to combine signs in order to create semiotic text that can convey meaning adequately.

Semiotics is the study of signs and symbols and how they are used in representing meaning, as 'a general philosophical theory of signs and symbols that deals especially with their function in both artificially constructed and natural languages and comprises syntactics, semantics, and pragmatics' (Merriam-Webster's Learner's Dictionary, 2016).

Listening to conversations among content experts we often notice a trend to reformulate the statement under discussion by introducing alternative points-of-view, sometime encoded in alternative representations in different sign systems. For example, a conversation that originated as a strictly verbal exchange, may progress to include images, diagrams, equations, etc. each with its own running – spoken - commentary.

Sigel defined representational competence as the ability to conserve meaning across different specific representations; he introduced a metacognitive aspect into the definition of representational competence. 'Representational competence" refers to the individual's awareness and understanding that an instance can be represented in various forms and still retain its essential meaning' (Sigel, 1993; p. 142; see Sigel, 1970; Sigel & Cocking, 1977).

According to the Russian psychologist Vygotsky 'It is the meaning that is important, not the sign. We can change the sign, but retain the meaning' (1930/1984; p. 74). The important role of representational competence in learning has been clearly documented in numerous developmental studies. In summarizing available experimental results, Case et al. (1996, p. 86) concluded that the development of children's conceptual thought is facilitated by representational diversity – the use of 'a variety of external forms of representation'. Commenting on coding meaning in mathematical science, Duval (2006, p. 107) described the role of mathematical systems of representation as 'no kind of mathematical processing can be performed without using a semiotic system of representation, because mathematical processing always involves substituting some semiotic representation for another', and emphasized the fact that mathematical objects are not directly accessible. 'Mathematical objects… are never accessible by perception or by instruments. The only way to have access to them and deal with them is using signs and semiotic representations…. Any learner is faced with two quite opposite requirements for getting into mathematical thinking:

- In order to do any mathematical activity, semiotic representations must necessarily be used even if there is the choice of the kind of semiotic representation.
- But the mathematical objects must never be confused with the semiotic representations that are used.'

Taking this discussion on representation even further, we can say that representational competence is the ability to trans-code meaning in a polymorphous - one-to-many - transformation of the representation of the meaning of a particular conceptual situation, through multiple representations within and across sign systems (Shafrir, 2012; Sternberg & Ben-Zeev, 1996).

Analysis of a sign system can only be accomplished by a formal description through a sign system - a metalanguage - that may or may not be identical to the system under analysis. A natural language is a sign system that may be analyzed by using it as a metalanguage; however, not every sign system may be used as a metalanguage for the description and analysis of itself or of other sign systems. For example, English is habitually used to describe and analyze musical codes, but a musical code cannot be used to describe and analyze English text (e.g., Simon & Sumner, 1968). From a developmental perspective, the crucial point is that in order to establish equivalence of meaning between two representations, one has to use a sign system that can act as a metalanguage with respect to both.

The Soviet semiotician Lotman who, together with Ivanov (1977/1965), organized and led the Tartu-Moscow school of semiotics between the early 1960s and the mid-1980s, pointed out the evolutionary nature of sign systems and the dynamic nature of their interactions across historical epochs as well as at any given historical moment (Lotman, 1990). In parallel to the evolutionary concept of an ever-changing, evolving biosphere, Lotman proposed the concept of a 'semiosphere' as the total symbolic environment of the individual and the collective. For Lotman the static definition of text as a semiotic corpus that conveys meaning does not capture its essentially dynamic nature: 'A Text is a semiotic space in which languages interact, interfere, and organize themselves hierarchically' (Lotman, 1981/1988, p. 37). Lotman described the semiotic text as serving three separate functions: (a) univocality - the transmission of meaning; (b) dialogic—the creation of new meaning: 'the text is a generator of meaning, a thinking device, which requires an interlocutor to be activated' (p. 40); and (c) memory - encoding the past within the semiotic text. This multifunctional view of the semiotic text has profound implications for development. For example, Wertch and Bivens (1993) claimed that the tendency to pay attention mostly to the univocal function of text - the transmission of meaning, at the expense of dialogic function - the generation of meaning - obstructs an important aspect of the text as catalyzer of internalization of socially mediated procedures.

The semiosphere is the symbolic environment that defines the types of representations to be encoded in the developing mind. The semiosphere is dynamic and multifunctional; it also includes a class of meaning-preserving transformations. These symbolic transformations generate multiple representations with equivalent meaning, and inevitably result in the over-determination of meaning within the semiosphere. A corollary of this aspect of the semiosphere is that the developing child is exposed, continuously and simultaneously, to multiple models of the world. The child may therefore interact, at any time, with any given aspect of the world through multiple representations (signifiers) that, nevertheless, preserve equivalent meanings. The ability of the developing child to represent experience - to model the world - in a multitude of ways lies at the core of the developmental construct 'representational competence' (Shafrir, 2012).

Definition of Representational Competence

The conceptual definition of representational competence has undergone considerable change since it was first formulated by Sigel (1954) in response to Osgood's (1952) claim that 'meanings are quite independent of the stimulus characteristics of the signs themselves' (p. 206). Sigel proposed that 'meaning of an object is not only independent of the stimulus characteristics of the object itself, but is also apparently dominant as a basis of organization of the objects. Meaning dominance is the term we suggest to apply to this phenomenon' (p. 207).

Later, Sigel and his collaborators (Sigel, 1970; Sigel & Cocking, 1977) defined representational competence as the ability to conserve meaning across different specific representations. Sigel (1993) introduced a metacognitive aspect into the definition of representational competence: 'Representational competence refers to the individual's awareness and understanding that an instance can be represented in various forms and still retain its essential meaning' (p. 142).

The construct 'representational competence' evolved in early research that focus on the concept 'meaning' in the latter half of the 20 century (Lotman, 1990; Osgood's, 1952; Sigel, 1954; 1970; Sigel & Cocking, 1977), namely, interpretation of concepts through equivalent expressions. Our definition consists of two hierarchical levels: In *Level 1* representational competence is conceptualized as the ability to convey and receive equivalent meaning through multiple representations within and/or across different sign systems; in *Level 2* representational competence is defined as the ability to re-represent equivalent meaning by incorporating higher order relations within and/or across different sign systems.

The first level requires that an individual is able to recognize and describe equivalent meanings embedded in at least two different representations in one or more sign systems. An individual who possesses a good Level 1 representational competence may be able to represent equivalent meanings in natural language, as well as through other sign systems (e.g., arithmetic, musical notation, charts, spatial projections, Morse code).

The second - and higher - level of representational competence requires that the individual is able to re-represent an equivalent meaning by encoding sub/superordinate relations; for example, by using linguistic descriptions of higher order concepts, or by incorporating additional aspects or relations that were not encoded into the initial representation, re-representation of equivalent meaning in terms of higher order relations.

The rationale for our definition of representational competence rests on two main arguments that may be summarized as follows. First, the over-determination of meaning in the semiosphere - the great number of possible different representations for conveying a specific meaning - suggests that the ability to model reality in multiple ways is an important prerequisite for development and learning. Stated differently, multiple representations may capture multiple aspects of the phenomena being represented and therefore facilitate comprehension. The second argument stems from the difficulty of making a judgment about the nature of a representation in another person's mind. Because representation is a mental construction that cannot be directly observed it seems that judgments by an external observer regarding the nature of an internal representation in another person's mind can be rendered only on the basis of some overt behavior of that person that is assumed to reflect (to signify), in the opinion of the observer, the existence of that representation. Such judgmental mappings of behaviors on hypothesized inner representations are notoriously difficult to make. By introducing the concept of meaning equivalence, we provide the observer with a strategy - making relative rather than absolute judgments - that is expected to facilitate the task of evaluating the nature of internal representations. Finally, we note that our definition of representational competence is applicable across ages and we present evidence on representational competence of adolescents and adults.

The following experiments were designed to explore different operational derivatives of this conceptual definition. In Experiment 1 we investigated the ability of university students to recognize meaning equivalence in printed text (Level 1). In Experiment 2 we studied the ability of 9- to 12-year-olds to spontaneously shift from an initial representation of an inference task to a superordinate re-representation of the same task that includes differential-valence feedback (Level 2).

Experiment 1: Representational Competence of Printed Text

Experiment 1 was designed to evaluate representational competence of printed text by asking university students to recognize meaning equivalence among several sentences. In this study Shalit (2006) examined the relationship between the representational competence of text and both low level reading skills (e.g., single-word decoding) and high-level reading skills (e.g., reading comprehension) in two groups of university students: reading disabled (RD) and normal readers (NR). We were particularly interested in the ability of these students to distinguish between the two levels of representation involved in text comprehension, namely, the surface level (e.g., the morphological appearance of a sentence), and the deeper level of the meaning conveyed by the text. This is a specific application, in the domain of reading, of our definition of representational competence - Level 1. Here we operationalized representational competence of text as the ability to recognize meaning equivalence in text samples that varied syntactically or grammatically.

Procedures

The 40 subjects were students at a university in Ontario, Canada. Twelve of these students reported that they were having problems with the reading of course material and that they experienced reading problems in elementary school; they also scored below the 50th percentile on the Woodcock Word Attack test. These students formed the RD group in this study (six men, six women; mean age 25.4 years, SD = 4.5). A non-selected control group of 28 university students who were NR (13 men and 15 women; mean age 24.3 years, SD = 3.1) volunteered to participate in this study.

The main task was a 10-item pencil-and-paper test of representational competence of text (RCT). Each item contained five sentences. The subject was told that at least two of the five sentences mean the same thing, but that possibly more than two sentences may mean the same thing, and was asked to mark all the same-meaning sentences among the group of five sentences for each item. In addition to the main task and the Woodcock Word Attack, each subject was administered the following tests: WAIS-R (Wechsler Adult Intelligence Scale-Revised); WRAT-R (Wide Range Achievement Test-Revised; reading); GORTR (Gray Oral Reading Tests-Revised); and the Nelson-Denny Test (reading comprehension). The procedure for administering the Nelson-Denny was as follows: After the normed time of 20 minutes, the answer sheet was marked and the subject was told that he or she may continue for as long as they need in order to complete the test. This procedure yielded the following measures: Score (in percentile) at 20 minutes; score (in percentile) at own time; and own time (minutes).

Results and Discussion

In addition to the two ability groups, we divided the population into two groups by the level of RCT; the low group scored 3 or below (n = 14) and included 8 RD and 6 NR; and the high group scored 4 or above on the RCT (n = 26) and included 4 RD and 22 NR (x^2 = 7.56, p < .006). A three-way analysis of variance (ANOVA), ability group (RD and NR), level of RCT (low and high), and score on Nelson-Denny (at 20 minutes and at own time) with a repeated measure on the scores on Nelson-Denny, showed a main effect for time (F(1,39) = 27.43, p < .0001); and for RCT (F(1,38) = 4.1, p < .05 (all results reported for Type III SS); but not for ability group; there were no interactions. A two-way ANOVA, ability group (RD and NR) by level of RCT (low and high) for GORT-R (reading quotient) showed a main effect for ability group (F= 5.73, p < .02), but not for RCT. No interaction was found.

Because we conceptualized representational competence as the ability to represent experience in alternative ways and operationalized it, in this study, as the ability to recognize meaning-equivalence in printed text, it can be argued that our measure of RCT is (a) just another test of reading comprehension; or, alternatively, (b) a new type of general ability, a sort of surrogate-IQ measure. The commonality analysis shows that RCT accounted for a significant amount of unique variance only for Nelson-Denny (own time) but not for GORT-R (where IQ accounted for a large portion of unique variance) or for Nelson-Denny at 20 minutes (where single-word decoding accounted for a large portion of unique variance). Of the three tests of reading comprehension, only the Nelson-Denny (own time) captured the maximal level of performance (for details, see: Shafrir, 2012).

Our interpretation of this analysis is that RCT is not just another measure of reading comprehension or a correlate of IQ, but that it is a measure of the ability to recognize equivalence in meaning among text samples that may vary along syntactic and grammatical dimensions. This corresponds to representational competence— Level 1. This interpretation is further supported by the results of the ANOVAs. It is also supported by recent studies by Royer and his collaborators (Royer, Greene, & Sinatra, 1987; Royer & Sinatra, 1994), who administered a procedure based on equivalence of meaning, known as the sentence verification technique (SVT) for assessing reading comprehension, to children and adolescents in the age range third grade to college. They found that the test is a good measure of paragraph comprehension, has high reliability, and has good construct validity. The studies of SVT by Royer and his collaborators showed that paraphrasing offers a good method to establish meaning equivalence between two sentences. Our exploratory study showed that RCT is an important measure that captures a fundamental aspect of development that is different from the general level of intellectual functioning on one hand, and from domain-specific expertise in reading on the other.

Experiment 2: Representational Competence in an Inference Task

The nature of inductive inference has long been a source of disagreements among philosophers, logicians, psychologists, and – recently - information processing and artificial intelligence theorists. However, most have recognized the centrality of inductive inference as a process that provides clues for action in unfamiliar circumstances, that may test the adequacy of rules in the stored knowledge base, and that allows knowledge to be transformed and modified through its use (see: Butler & Markman, 2014; Margolis & Laurence, 2008).

An inference task may be defined as a learning task where response is followed by feedback, which is the main source of learning. An important potential source of information in an inference task is the valence of the feedback. Whereas positive feedback simply confirms the adequacy of the response, negative feedback signals the presence of flaws in the mental procedures that guided the subject's response. Therefore, paying attention to negative feedback may be expected to play an important role in improving performance on inferential tasks.

Paying attention to errors, signaled by negative feedback on an inference task, was operationalized recently by the measure of post-failure reflectivity (Shafrir, 2012). Post-failure reflective children spend long periods of time following the production of incorrect response, compared to the time they spend following the production of correct response. Post-failure reflectivity is an exploratory mental executive, a spontaneously activated "debugging" procedure that helps children re-examine and correct faulty internal plans.

Research (Shafrir, Ogilvie & Bryson, 1990) show that:

- Children who spent a lot of time contemplating errors (post-failure reflective children), scored higher than post-failure impulsive children on an inference task as well as on other measures of intellectual functioning and academic achievement

- Post-failure reflectivity generalized across tasks and across domains
- Post-failure reflective children were intentional learners and good planners
- Paying attention to errors plays an important role in learning

In Experiment 2 (Shafrir, 2012) we shed light on representational competence - Level 2. We reasoned that because task instructions did not mention feedback and did not mention the need to pay attention to negative feedback children who did pay attention to such feedback did so spontaneously by re-representing the task. They moved from an initial task representation based on the need to respond to the immediate features of the stimulus in a given trial, to a re-representation of the task that included, in addition to the stimulus, also the response, and the valence of the feedback to the response in the current trial. Children who spontaneously change their task representation to include both potential and actual negative feedback on an inference task, demonstrate Level 2 of representational competence.

The two specific hypotheses tested in this study are:

1. 12-year-olds spontaneously produce re-representations that include the valence of the immediate feedback, and score higher on an inference task as well as on other intellectual and academic tasks than younger children.
2. Within each of the four age groups tested (9,10,11, and 12 years old), children who spontaneously produce task re-representations that include both potential and actual negative feedback on an inference task, score higher than children who do not produce such re-representations, as well as on other intellectual and academic tasks.

Procedures

Subjects were students in grades 4 through 7 in public schools in Israel. We tested an unselected sample of 377 subjects, aged 9 (n = 109), 10 (n = 114), 11 (n = 85), and 12 (n = 69).

Scores for the Israeli version of an IQ test (M = 106.1, SD = 11.5), and for Raven's (1960) Standard Progressive Matrices (SPM; M= 32.5, SD= 8.6), were obtained when children entered third grade. Scores for computer-based drill and practice in arithmetic, and for teachers' evaluations of the student's general level of intellectual functioning (not level of academic achievement) in percentiles, were available at the time of this study. The Figural Intersection

Test (FIT) for mental attentional capacity (M) was group administered. The PAR (Pattern Recognition) task was administered individually.

PAR is a computer-based inference task, with 80 stimuli of repeated designs shown through bars of different colors; heights; colors + heights; and colors + heights + sounds of varying pitch, where inter-trial intervals are subject controlled. Subjects were asked to decide whether the stimulus was a 'repeating design'. If the subject's answer was 'no', he or she was asked to point to the location of the 'mistake' in the design with a blinking light on the computer screen. Response was immediately followed by positive feedback ('yes, you are right') or negative feedback ('no, you are wrong'); the subject had to strike a key in order to continue and see the next stimulus.

The response latency was classified into two mutually exclusive classes, that is, pre-success and pre-failure; similarly, the post-response latency was classified as post-success and post-failure. Pre-failure and post-failure reflectivities were calculated from equations 1 and 2, as follows:

$$Pre-failure\ reflectivity = \frac{Mean\ pre-failure\ latency}{Mean\ response\ latency} \tag{1}$$

$$Post-failure\ reflectivity = \frac{Mean\ post-failure\ latency}{Mean\ post-response\ latency} \tag{2}$$

Children in each age group were divided by a double median split on pre-failure reflectivity and on post-failure reflectivity, into four quadrants: children who were both pre- and post-failure reflective were assumed to have spontaneously produced a re-representation of the inference task that includes potential and actual negative feedback; these children were conceptualized as having high Level 2 representational competence. Children who were both pre- and post-failure impulsive were conceptualized as not having developed such a re-representation and therefore as having low Level 2 representational competence; finally, there were two groups of mixed conditions.

Results and Discussion

Results of 2-way ANOVAs, age (four levels: 9, 10, 11, and 12 years old) by Level 2 representational competence (four levels: high, low, and two mixed conditions), showed that 12-year-olds scored significantly higher on the

FIT task for attentional capacity, showed higher Level 2 representational competence (were more pre-failure as well as more post-failure reflective) than children in the 9 to 11 years age range; the 12-year-olds also scored higher on PAR. Within each age group, children with high Level 2 representational competence performed better on the PAR task, scored significantly higher on a variety of tasks of intellectual functioning, on teacher's evaluations of intellectual functioning, and on arithmetic drill and practice, than children with low Level 2 representational competence. The two groups of mixed conditions scored in the intermediate range. The younger children in the 9 and 10 years old age groups with high Level 2 representational competence scored as high as the 12-year-olds on a measure of attentional capacity (a score of 5 on the FIT task). These younger children scored significantly higher on the various tasks than the children in the 12 years old age group who had low Level 2 representational competence.

Finally, we performed a commonality analysis of the variance of the score on PAR as the dependent variable, and age, FIT, IQ, SPM, math, and pre- and post-failure reflectivities as the independent variables (teachers' evaluations were available for only 252 children and were not included in this analysis). The unique contribution of the Level 2 representational competence (pre- and post-failure reflectivities) to the variance of the score on the PAR inference task was higher (about 15%) than the unique contributions of all of the other independent variables combined: age (2.3%), M-capacity (0.8%), IQ (2.7%), SPM (0.6%), and arithmetic drill and practice (0.0%).

These results lend support to the two hypotheses. The significant increase in Level 2 representational competence at age 12 corresponds to an increase of attentional capacity from four to five units as predicted by Pascual-Leone (1987), and to the onset of the stage of formal operations (Piaget, 1950), vectorial operations (Case, 1985), and abstract sets (Fischer, 1980). The newly acquired ability of 12-year-old children to operate on operations, and not only on concrete entities, facilitates the development of Level 2 representational competence - to spontaneously produce a re-representation that includes, in addition to the task itself, the differential-valence feedback, and possibly also concomitant internal procedures that "debug" and improve currently operating action plans. This ability also incorporates an important affective component: attending to one's own errors requires the retracing of mental steps and a re-examination of one's plans that turned sour - contained faulty elements. In other words, post-failure reflective behavior is predicated on the ability to concentrate and draw conclusions from environmentally driven negative feedback under conditions of affective adversity. The adaptive advantage derived from such competence may be reflected during development in acquiring the ability to incorporate negative feedback into representations of inference tasks.

The longer periods of time that 12-year-olds spent both prior to as well as following production of incorrect response, compared to the time they spent prior to - as well as following - the production of correct response, appear to signal the emergence of this higher level of representational competence that incorporates differential-valence feedback, and that results in an emphasis on optimizing performance.

SOLUTIONS AND RECOMMENDATIONS

We believe that the over-determination of meaning in the semiosphere plays a central role in development. It stems from the concurrent availability of a multitude of ways to represent experience by constructing different representations within a sign system, as well as across different sign systems.

Representational competence is the ability to model important features of the world in different ways while maintaining equivalence of meaning. This means that a high degree of representational competence allows to decode and to encode experience differently, and in more ways, than a low degree of representational competence. The richer mode of interaction with environmental inputs can be expected to result in differential rates of learning and development.

We provide support for this claim by summarizing the results of our two studies presented earlier. Results of Experiment 1 showed that the ability to recognize equivalence of meaning of printed text contributed unique variance only to a test of reading comprehension that was designed to elicit maximal results (e.g., Nelson-Denny, own time), but not to two other tests that put various constraints on the demonstration of reading comprehension (e.g., Nelson-Denny at 20 minutes, and GORT-R). The pattern of contribution of unique variance to three different tests of reading comprehension was different than the patterns of contribution of unique variance of two other independent variables, namely, single-word decoding and IQ. University students who reported having reading problems beginning at an early age, and who showed deficits in nonword decoding that are often associated with a core phonological deficit (Stanovich & Siegel, 1994), did not score uniformly low on representational competence of text. Similarly, an unselected group of university students who did not report having reading problems did not score uniformly high on representational competence of text. Representational competence of printed text seems to reflect a dimension of reading that is different from reading ability (e.g., single-word decoding) on one hand, and from IQ on the other. These results support our view that representational competence is an important mediator of learning.

Results of Experiment 2 showed that the ability to spontaneously re-represent an inference task, where the "new" representation incorporates the superordinate relations of differential-valence feedback as well as debugging routines, is associated with higher intellectual functioning and higher academic achievement. This finding held across the four age groups (e.g., 9 to 12 years old), but was more pronounced for the 12-year-olds.

The relationship between Level 2 representational competence and development is illuminated by examining it vis-à-vis three other measures administered in Experiment 2. High ability to spontaneously re-represent an inference task while incorporating higher order relations successfully postdicted - for all four age groups - high scores on IQ and RPM, the two main measures of intellectual functioning, that were obtained between 1 and 4 years prior to the time of Experiment 2. Representational competence is a self-sustaining mechanism that propels development and learning.

CONCLUSION

The conclusions described above should be viewed in context of recent studies of learning with multiple representations, and of neural representation of concepts in the brain; here are brief descriptions of three samples of such studies:

'Multiple (external) representations can provide unique benefits when people are learning complex new ideas. Unfortunately, many studies have shown this promise is not always achieved. The DeFT (Design, Functions, Tasks) framework for learning with multiple representations integrates research on learning, the cognitive science of representation and constructivist theories of education. It proposes that the effectiveness of multiple representations can best be understood by considering three fundamental aspects of learning: the design parameters that are unique to learning with multiple representations; the functions that multiple representations serve in supporting learning and the cognitive tasks that must be undertaken by a learner interacting with multiple representations. The utility of this framework is proposed to be in identifying a broad range of factors that influence learning, reconciling inconsistent experimental findings, revealing under-explored areas of multi-representational research and pointing forward to potential design heuristics for learning with multiple representations.' (Ainsworth, 2006).

'Interaction with everyday objects requires the representation of conceptual object properties, such as where and how an object is used. What are the neural mechanisms that support this knowledge? While research on semantic dementia has provided evidence for a critical role of the anterior temporal lobes (ATLs) in object knowledge, fMRI studies using univariate analysis have primarily implicated regions outside the ATL. In the present human fMRI study we used multivoxel pattern analysis to test whether activity patterns in ATLs carry information about conceptual object properties. Participants viewed objects that differed on two dimensions: where the object is typically found (in the kitchen or the garage) and how the object is commonly used (with a rotate or a squeeze movement). Anatomical region-of-interest analyses covering the ventral visual stream revealed that information about the location and action dimensions increased from posterior to anterior ventral temporal cortex, peaking in the temporal pole. Whole-brain multivoxel searchlight analysis confirmed these results, revealing highly significant and regionally specific information about the location and action dimensions in the anterior temporal lobes bilaterally. In contrast to conceptual object properties, perceptual and low-level visual properties of the objects were reflected in activity patterns in posterior lateral occipitotemporal cortex and occipital cortex, respectively. These results provide fMRI evidence that object representations in the anterior temporal lobes are abstracted away from perceptual properties, categorizing objects in semantically meaningful groups to support conceptual object knowledge.' (Peelen & Caramazza, 2012).

'Recent research indicates that sensory and motor cortical areas play a significant role in the neural representation of concepts. However, little is known about the overall architecture of this representational system, including the role played by higher level areas that integrate different types of sensory and motor information. The present study addressed this issue by investigating the simultaneous contributions of multiple sensory-motor modalities to semantic word processing. With a multivariate fMRI design, we examined activation associated with 5 sensory-motor attributes—color, shape, visual motion, sound, and manipulation—for 900 words. Regions responsive to each attribute were identified using independent ratings of the attributes' relevance to the meaning of each word. The results indicate that these aspects of conceptual knowledge are encoded in multimodal and higher level unimodal areas involved in processing the corresponding types of information during perception and action, in agreement with embodied theories of semantics. They also reveal a hierarchical system of abstracted sensorymotor representations incorporating a major division between object interaction and object perception processes.' (Ferdinando et. al, 2016).

REFERENCES

Ainsworth, S. (2006). DeFT: A conceptual framework for considering learning with multiple representations. Elsevier. *Learning and Instruction*, *16*(3), 183–198. doi:10.1016/j.learninstruc.2006.03.001

Bever, T. G. (1986). The aesthetic basis for cognitive structures. In M. Brand & R. M. Harnish (Eds.), *The representation of knowledge and belief* (pp. 314–356). Tucson: University of Arizona Press.

Butler, L. P., & Markman, E. M. (2014). Preschoolers use pedagogical cues to guide radical reorganization of category knowledge. *Cognition*, *130*(1), 116–127. doi:10.1016/j.cognition.2013.10.002 PMID:24211439

Case, R., & Okamoto, Y. (1996). The Role of Central Conceptual Structures in the Development of Children's Thought. Monographs of the Society for Research in Child Development. *Serial*, *61*(216), 1–2.

Cocking, R. R. (2012). Introduction. In I.E. Sigel (Ed.), *Development of mental representation*, (pp. 3-12). NJ: Lawrence Erlbaum Associates, Inc.

Darwin, C. (1877). A biographical sketch of an infant. *Mind*, *7*(7), 285–294. doi:10.1093/mind/os-2.7.285

DeLoache, J. S. (1993). Distancing and dual representation. In R. R. Cocking & K. A. Renninger (Eds.), *The development and meaning of psychological distance* (pp. 91–107). Hillsdale, NJ: Lawrence Erlbaum Associates.

Dudai, Y. (1989). *The neurobiology of memory: Concepts, findings, trends.* Oxford, England: Oxford University Press.

Duval, R. (2006). A cognitive analysis of problems of comprehension in a learning of mathematics. *Educational Studies in Mathematics*, *61*(1-2), 103–131. doi:10.1007/s10649-006-0400-z

Eco, U. (1976). *A theory of semiotics*. Bloomington: Indiana University Press. doi:10.1007/978-1-349-15849-2

Etkind, M., Kenett, R. S., & Shafrir, U. (2016). Learning in the Digital Age with Meaning Equivalence Reusable Learning Objects (MERLO). In Railean, E., Walker, G., Elçi, A., & Jackson, L. (Eds.), *Handbook of Research on Applied Learning Theory and Design in Modern Education,* pp. 310-333, Hershey, PA: IGI Global.

Fernandino, L., Binder, J. R., Desai, R. H., Pendl, S. L., Humphries, C. J., Gross, W. L., & Seidenberg, M. S. et al. (2016). Concept Representation Reflects Multimodal Abstraction: A Framework for Embodied Semantics. *Cerebral Cortex*, *26*(5), 2018–2034. doi:10.1093/cercor/bhv020 PMID:25750259

Gotts, S. J. (2016). Incremental learning of perceptual and conceptual representations and the puzzle of neural repetition suppression. *Springer. Psychon. Bull. Rev.*, *23*(4), 1055–1071. doi:10.3758/s13423-015-0855-y PMID:27294423

Gotts, S. J., Milleville, S. C., & Martin, A. (2014). Object identification leads to a conceptual broadening of object representations in lateral prefrontal cortex. *Neuropsychologia.* doi:10.1016/j.neuropsychologia.2014.10.041 PMID:25445775

Ivanov, V. V. (1977). The role of semiotics in the cybernetic study of man and collective. In D. P. Lucid (Ed.), *Soviet Semiotics* (pp. 27–38). Baltimore: John Hopkins University Press. (Original work published 1965)

Lotman, Y. M. (1988). Text within a text. Soviet Psychology, 26, 32-51. (Original work published 1981).

Lotman, Y. M. (1990). *Universe of the mind: A semiotic theory of culture.* Bloomington: Indiana University Press.

Margolis, E., & Laurence, S. (2008). How to learn the natural numbers: Inductive inference and the acquisition of number concepts. *Cognition*, *106*(2), 924–939. doi:10.1016/j.cognition.2007.03.003 PMID:17482155

McLelland, J. L. (1995). A connectionist perspective on knowledge and development. In T. J. Simon & G. S. Hallford (Eds.), *Developing cognitive competence: New approaches to process modelling* (pp. 157–204). Hillsdale, NJ: Lawrence Erlbaum Associates.

Meltzoff, A. N., & Moore, M. K. (1994). Imitation, memory, and the representation of persons. *Infant Behavior and Development, 17*(1), 83–89. doi:10.1016/0163-6383(94)90024-8 PMID:25147416

Merriam - Webster's Learner's Dictionary. (2016). *Encyclopaedia Britannica*. London.

Osgood, C. E. (1952). The nature and measurement of meaning. *Psychological Bulletin, 49*(3), 197–237. doi:10.1037/h0055737 PMID:14930159

Peelen, M. V., & Caramazza, A. (2012). Conceptual Object Representations in Human Anterior Temporal Cortex. *The Journal of Neuroscience, 32*(45), 15728–15736. doi:10.1523/JNEUROSCI.1953-12.2012 PMID:23136412

Royer, J. M., Greene, B. A., & Sinatra, G. M. (1987). The sentence verification technique: A practical procedure teachers can use to develop their own reading and listening comprehension tests. *Journal of Reading, 340*, 414–423.

Royer, J. M., & Sinanta, G. M. (1994). A cognitive developmental approach to reading diagnostics. *Educational Psychology Review, 6*(2), 81–113. doi:10.1007/BF02208969

Shafrir, U. (2012). Representational competence. In I. E. Sigel (Ed.), *The Development of Mental Representation: Theory and Applications.* (pp. 371-389). Mahwah, NJ: Lawrence Erlbaum Publishers.

Shafrir, U., & Etkind, M. (2006). eLearning for depth in the semantic web. *British Journal of Educational Technology, 37*(3), 425–444. doi:10.1111/j.1467-8535.2006.00614.x

Shafrir, U., & Kenett, R. S. (2016). Concept Science Evidence Based MERLO Learning Analytics. In Railean, E., Walker, G., Elçi, A., & Jackson, L. (Eds.), *Handbook of Research on Applied Learning Theory and Design in Modern Education,* pp. 334-357, Hershey, PA: IGI Global. doi:10.4018/978-1-4666-9634-1.ch016

Shafrir, U., Ogilvie, M., & Bryson, M. (1990). Attention to errors and learning: Across-task and across-domain analysis of the post-failure reflectivity measure. *Cognitive Development, 5*(4), 405–425. doi:10.1016/0885-2014(90)90005-E

Sigel, I. E. (1954). The dominance of meaning. *The Journal of Genetic Psychology, 85*(2), 201–207. doi:10.1080/00221325.1954.10532876 PMID:13221783

Sigel, I. E. (1970). The distancing hypothesis: A causal hypothesis for the acquisition of representational thought. In M. R. Jones (Ed.), *Miami symposium on the prediction of behavior, 1968: Effect of early experiences* (pp. 99–118). Coral Gables, FL: University of Miami Press.

Sigel, I. E. (1986). Early social experience and the development of representational competence. In W. Fowler (Ed.), *Early experience and the development of competence* (pp. 49–65). San Francisco: Jossey-Bass. doi:10.1002/cd.23219863205

Sigel, I. E. (1993). The centrality of a distancing model for the development of representational competence. In R. R. Cocking & K. A. Renninger (Eds.), *The development and meaning of psychological distance* (pp. 141–158).

Sigel, I. E. (2012). Approaches to representation as a psychological construct: a treatise in diversity. In I.E. Sigel (Ed.), *Development of mental representation*, (pp. 3-12). NJ: Lawrence Erlbaum Associates, Inc.

Sigel, I. E., Anderson, L. M., & Shapiro, H. (1966). Categorization behavior of lower and middle class Negro preschool children: Differences in dealing with representation of familiar objects. *The Journal of Negro Education*, *35*(3), 218–229. doi:10.2307/2293941

Sigel, I. E., & Cocking, R. R. (1977). Cognition and communication: A dialectic paradigm for devel- opment. In M. Lewis & L. A. Rosenblum (Eds.), *The origins of behavior: Vol. 5. Indexation, conversation, and the development of language* (pp. 207-226). New York: Wiley.

Sigel, I. E., & McBane, B. (1967). Cognitive competence and level of symbolization among five-yearold children. In J. Hellmuth (Ed.), *The disadvantaged child* (Vol. I, pp. 433–453). Seattle: Special Child Publications of the Seattle Sequin School.

Sigel, I. E., & Olmstead, P. (1970a). The development of classification and representational competence. In A. J. Biemiller (Ed.), *Problems in the teaching of young children* (pp. 49–67). Toronto: OISE Press.

Sigel, I. E., & Olmstead, P. (1970b). Modification of cognitive skills among lower-class Black children. In J. Hellmuth (Ed.), *The disadvantaged child* (Vol. 3, pp. 300–338). New York: Brunner-Mazel.

Simon, H. A., & Sumner, R. K. (1968). Pattern in music. In B. Kleinmuntz (Ed.), *Formal representation of human judgement* (pp. 219–250). New York: Wiley.

Stanovich, K. E., & Siegel, L. S. (1994). Phenotypic performance profile of children with reading disabilities: A regression-based test of the phonological-core variable-difference model. *Journal of Educational Psychology, 86*(1), 24–53. doi:10.1037/0022-0663.86.1.24

Sternberg, R. J., & Ben Zeev, T. (1996). *The Nature of Mathematical Thinking*. Mahwah, NJ: Lawrence Erlbaum.

Vygotsky, L. S. (1930/1984). Orudie i znak v razvitii rebĕnka (Tool and sign in the development of the child), in L. S. Vygodsky, Sobranye Socinenij, Volume 6, pp. 6-90 (Collected Works, 6; Pedagogika, originally published 1930).

Vygotsky, L. S. (1978). *Mind in society: The development of higher psychological processes*. Cambridge, MA: Harvard University Press.

Wertsch, J. V., & Bivens, J. A. (1993). The social origins of intellectual mental functioning: Alternatives and perspectives. In R. R. Cocking & K. A. Renninger (Eds.), *The development and meaning of psychological distance* (pp. 203–218). Hillsdale, NJ: Lawrence Erlbaum Associates.

Chapter 2
Natural Language and Sub-Languages with Controlled Vocabularies

ABSTRACT

This chapter describe differences between natural languages and special-purpose languages, where certain words used to describe observed regularities and patterns, acquire over time specific meanings that differ from their 'ordinary' meanings in the language. Folk taxonomies, encoded in languages of peoples who occupy narrow ecological niches, serve an existential need of encoding knowledge important for survival. While folk biology developed taxonomies based on the human sensory system, modern biology evolves by including observational data from molecular biology collected with modern bio-chemical tools – scientific 'extensions' of the human sensory system. In contrast to general language, the controlled vocabulary in 'specialist discourse', also referred to by linguists as 'sublanguage' and 'Language for Special Purposes' (LSP) allows specialists to communicate in precisely defined terms and to avoid ambiguity in discussing specific conceptual situations

DOI: 10.4018/978-1-5225-2176-1.ch002

INTRODUCTION

In addition to the common use of language for everyday communications, a group of specialists can use the same language to encode and to communicate the encoded knowledge. As traced by Bloomfield (1938) the development and use of encoded language goes back to early division of labor and development of specializations in practical occupations such as carpentry, fishing, etc. The very nature of such specializations was rooted in careful observations of made by early humans that eventually resulted in awareness and recognition of certain patterns in the environment: Some fish travel in schools; follow certain weather patterns; certain fish are prone to be caught with certain bait.

Let us tell you a story that illustrates the difference in conceptual comprehension between two competent users of natural language. Imagine an expert in discipline X –name him EX, who invites his friend, a competent user of their common language – name him CU, to attend a lecture given by a colleague who happens to be a famous scholar in knowledge domain X. As the two leave the room following the lecture, EX asks CU "Did you get what he was talking about? I found his ideas exciting!" To which CU replies "Oh yes, I got it! I actually understood every word he said."

We can imagine the concluding episode to this story. Upon quick questioning by EX it turned out that his friend CU did not really follow the speaker's ideas; furthermore, he did not understand that certain expressions – word sequences – used by the speaker, carried meanings that were significantly different from the literal meaning of those same expressions in the common use of the language.

What are we to make of this story?
Should we really be surprised that CU did not get the meaning of the talk?

After all, scholars often communicate complex theories through the use of common language (this is true not only in social sciences, but also in mathematics and exact science); CU's remark that he "understood every word" should not be surprising. On the other hand, we should also not be surprised that he failed to provide satisfactory answers to EX's probing questions: unlike his friend, CU is just a competent user of the language, not an expert in the discipline X. CU understood the words, but missed the ideas communicated in the talk.

Our story highlights a phenomenon familiar to many language users, namely, the coding of discipline-specific knowledge under the guise of lexical labels that are familiar words borrowed from natural common language. When used as lexical label for a specialized term, a familiar word changes its meaning, turns into a symbol of different connotation, and becomes a part of different semiotic system.

All disciplines use 'secret codes' to communicate meaning; this is what scientists and other professionals mean by 'shop talk': common construction of meaning by initiates who share the discipline's 'secret code'. It is easy to verify that such codes exist both in scientific disciplines as well as in the professions. Certain words, used to describe such regularities, acquire over time specific meanings that differ from their 'ordinary' meanings in the language. These 'code words' are like secret passages that lead to hidden stores of organized information: ways of conceptualizing an otherwise chaotic avalanche of undifferentiated facts. These words do not comprise a new language; rather, they are ordinary words used within a particular framework of the language to communicate special meanings: specific conceptual content in the context of the body of knowledge of a discipline, a profession, or a specialization. They originate from the common need to eliminate – at least reduce – ambiguity, and to define conceptual content in precise terms that allow clear demarcation between the known and the unknown.

MAIN FOCUS OF THE CHAPTER

Issues, Controversies, Problems

'…There's glory for you!'

'I don't know what you mean by "glory,"' Alice said.

Humpty Dumpty smiled contemptuously. 'Of course you don't - till I tell you. I mean "there's a nice knock-down argument for you!"'

'But "glory" doesn't mean "a nice knock-down argument,"' Alice objected.

*'When **I** use a word,' Humpty Dumpty said, in rather a scornful tone, 'it means just what **I** choose it to mean - neither more nor less.'*

*'The question is,' said Alice, 'whether you **can** make words mean so many different things.'*

'The question is,' said Humpty Dumpty, 'which is to be master - that's all.'

...'When I make a word do a lot of work like that,' said Humpty Dumpty, 'I always pay it extra.'

(Lewis Carroll, 1982, pp. 190-191)

What is 'Concept'?

Like Humpty Dumpty, scientists are masters of the meanings of the words they choose to describe observed phenomena in the universe.

Olson (1994, p. 228) describes the evolution of folk biology into the controlled vocabulary of scientific biology: 'Folk biological classifications of plants into flowers, fruits and vegetables are expressions of a social function – a fruit is something one eats for desert. Scientific botany sees the fruit from, so to speak, the plant's point of view, as an instrument of seed dispersion. The general theoretical scheme involves the attempt to integrate all botanical knowledge... It is this attempt... that turns folk biology into a science. The attempt to capture universal properties of plants by means of a proscribed set of distinguishing features, first in drawings and then in a technical descriptive vocabulary were important steps in that achievement'.

Folk taxonomies are encoded in languages of peoples who occupy narrow ecological niches, and serve an existential need of encoding knowledge important for survival. In his description of 'the extinction of the world's languages and the erosion of human knowledge' Harrison (2007) analyze the intrinsic survival value of naming differentiation 'The longer a particular people have inhabited and made use of an ecological niche and practiced a particular lifeway the more likely they will have applied their linguistic genius to describing that ecosystem... discerning the subtle connections, similarities, and behavioural traits linking animals, plants, and human demands careful observation over generations' (p. 25). Harrison then demonstrates his analysis in several case studies; for example, different types of reindeer distinguished by the Tofa reindeer herding people of Siberia: '*Dongur*. It is a powerful word. It means 'male domesticated reindeer in its third year and first mating season, but not ready for mating', and it allows a tribe of nomadic reindeer herders in Siberia to identify and describe with a single word what would otherwise require a full sentence' (p. 57).

Other examples describe seasonal time reckoning of the Kauli people of Papua New Guinea. Their calendar is not based on counting months or moons but on reading forest vegetation and naming the seasons by the appearance of birds or plants (p. 85). And detailed knowledge of rice of the Ifugao people of the Luzon mountains in the Philippines, encoded in differentiation of 'subtle qualities of rice stalks and grains: color, plumpness, texture, crunchiness', and in the special names of numerous utensils, products, and processes involved in rice growing (p. 162).

Knowledge encoded in indigenous languages is not limited to esoteric aspects of survival value of life in narrow environmental niches (Crystal, 2000; Nettle & Romaine, 2000). It is demonstrated by the physicist Peat (1996) who documented *'indigenous science'* by living with aboriginal native Americans at the Blackfoot Confederacy in western Canada. To his great surprise Peat discovered that this alternative science provide a comprehensive view of the universe and of humans' place in it and address such issues as 'the nature of space and time; the connection between language, thought, and perception; mathematics and its relationship to time; the ultimate nature of reality; causality and interconnection; astronomy and the movement of time; healing; the inner nature of animals, rocks and plants; … the importance of maintaining a balanced exchange of energy; of agriculture; of genetics;… and of the nature of processes of knowing' (p. xi). This universe contains interconnected, contextualized situations and, consequently, concepts that change with the situation: 'To create a category is to set a boundary within thought. It is to place a conceptual circumference around something. But, again, we must recall what the Blackfoot people say about their circles – they are always open, always ready to accept something new.' (p. 229). The category 'knife' in western languages denotes 'things used for cutting', but '…in the hunter's world all knives are individual' (p. 228). Dividing the meat of a killed caribou is not done by abstract concepts such as geometrical proportions, shapes, or even weight. Rather, the meat is divided by taking into account the physiological nature of each inner part of the animal, i.e., brains, tongue, rump, etc.; and the needs of the individual people who will receive portions: 'should an old man's portion weigh the same as a young hunter's?' (p. 229)

Archeology of the pre-historical origins of the concept of measurement explore the foundations of material culture, and the evolution of formal systems for counting; calendars; measuring time, distance and direction for navigation; weighing; architectural measurements of monuments, buildings and city planning (Morley & Renfrew, 2010, p. 2): 'Any notion of measure implies experience of the world in a more involved way. It involves also the notion of equivalence. For to measure some feature of the world means to compare it with some other feature of the world'. The complex relations of measures and meanings of objects in historical perspective is discussed by Godsen (2005): 'Decisions taken when making objects may occur without deliberate reflection on meaning, but never without some overall cognizance of the prevailing social context of material forms. One of the mysteries of things is that they take an infinity of forms, but often also have marked resemblances with one another, and the notion of style tries to probe the tension between similarity and difference which maintains and creates both.' (p. 196; see also Johannsen, Jessen, & Jensen, 2012).

SOLUTIONS AND RECOMMENDATIONS

Language describe *umwelt* (German for 'the environment') - the perceived world - and reflects human experience, needs to communicate, and needs for survival (Yoon, 2009). But meaning and relevance in *umwelt* changes with time (Wilson & Sperber, 2012). For example, while folk biology developed taxonomies based on the human sensory system, modern biology evolves by including observational data from molecular biology collected with modern bio-chemical tools – scientific 'extensions' of the human sensory system. Inconsistencies between name of patterns in folk- and in modern-biology as well as across different folk-biological taxonomies, evolved in various isolated societies, are described in detail and analyzed from both anthropological *and* psychological points-of-view in a fascinating book by Atran & Medin (2008[1]).

Controlled Vocabularies

In contrast to general language controlled vocabulary in 'specialist discourse' also referred to by linguists as 'sublanguage' and 'Language for Special Purposes' (LSP), allows specialists to communicate in precisely defined terms and to avoid ambiguity in discussing specific conceptual situations: 'In principle, any language could be used to formulate a theory, including extensions of everyday natural languages constructed through pragmatic observations of the linguistic usage within a scientific community' (Wang, 2007).

Kittredge (1983) described 'sublanguage' as restricted in four contexts. They are: (i) domain of reference; (ii) purpose and orientation; (iii) mode of communication; and (iv) the community of participants sharing specialized knowledge: 'The best, canonical examples of sublanguages are those for which there exists an identifiable community of users who share specialized knowledge and who communicate under restrictions of domain, purpose, and mode by using the sublanguage. These participants enforce the special patterns of usage and ensure the coherence and completeness of the sublanguage as a linguistic system' (p. 49).

'Code words' in a sublanguage do not comprise a new language; rather, code words (often nouns and noun phrases) are *lexical labels* of concepts. They are elements of a controlled vocabulary that encode conceptual content within a body of knowledge in a discipline, a profession, a domain. Lexical label acts as a proper name of a regularity; an organizing principle behind a collection of facts in context; an invariant; a pattern in the data. Lexical label is often one or more common words used to name a recognized pattern in human experience and to communicate a well defined meaning. 'Code words' are terms with very precise definition in one subject. Thus 'drift' and 'linkage' have quite special meanings for biologists, as does 'association' for psychologists, 'reference' for linguistic semanticists, and 'identity' and 'representation' for philosophers. In the most pernicious cases, the *same* term is used in different senses by different disciplines. Thus linguists and philosophers often mean different things by 'subject' and 'predicate' (Hurford, 2007, p. xiii).

Things can get even more confusing when the same word is not only 'used in different senses by different disciplines' – such as 'colour' in the context 'vision' in biology, and in the context 'electromagnetism' in physics – but is also used as lexical label of more than one concept in a particular discipline. Thus, the word 'color' is also used in context 'elementary particles' in physics as a lexical label of the concept of 'strong force'. However, not all concepts in particle physics have lexical labels that are common words; other concepts in particle physics are labelled 'quark' and 'gluon' – certainly not common English words.

Lexical Labels of Concepts

How are concepts - patterns in the data - encoded and communicated in the different disciplines? The use of 'code words' as lexical labels of concepts differs from the use of these same words in ordinary language in two important ways:

1. Lexical labels of concepts do not encode the literal meanings associated with their constituent words in the common use of the language; each such label encodes a connoted meaning, rooted in the regularity being considered, that differs from the literal meaning of the word(s).
2. Lexical labels of concepts cannot be replaced by synonyms; each label functions as a proper name of the signified concept.

Initiates – insiders who share the code - know that a lexical label of a concept serves a similar function to that of a proper name. On the other hand, when 'outsiders' encounter a lexical label, they do not associate it with discipline-specific meaning, and assume that the label is just a word in general language and therefore may be substituted by a synonym 'In general language it is easy to find synonymous expressions, but in specialist discourse the exact term for the conceptual equivalent is expected' (Sager, 1993, p. 226). This reflects Francis Bacon (1857-64) concerns regarding the dangers of ill-defined scientific terms: 'it is almost necessary, in all controversies and disputations, to imitate the wisdom of the mathematicians, in setting down in the very beginning the definitions of our words and terms, that others may know how we accept and understand them, and whether they concur with us or no. For it cometh to pass, for want of this, that we are sure to end there where we ought to have begun, which is in questions and differences about words' (quoted by Olson, 1994, p. 166).

The central role of regularities - patterns in the data - in specialist discourse in mathematics, is described by Devlin (1996, pp. 3-6): 'Mathematics is *the science of patterns*. What the mathematician does is examine abstract 'patterns' – numerical patterns, patterns of shape, patterns of motion, patterns of behavior, and so on. Those patterns can be either real or imagined, visual or mental, static or dynamic, qualitative or quantitative, purely utilitarian or little more than recreational interest. They can arise from the world around us, from the depths of space and time, or from the inner workings of the human mind... abstract patterns are the very essence of thought, of communication, of computation, of society, and of life itself'.

Each such pattern has a proper name, a lexical label in the sublanguage of mathematics: 'Mathematical discourse is multisemiotic because it involves the use of the semiotic resources of mathematical symbolism, visual display and language. There is constant movement between the three resources as the primary code and with shifts between spoken and written modes in classrooms. The complexity of pedagogical discourse arises because each of the three semiotic resources have their own unique lexicogrammatical systems for encoding meaning, and these interact to shape the nature of constructions found in the classroom. This is especially significant in the case of mathematical symbolism where meaning is encoded unambiguously in the most economical manner possible through specific grammatical strategies, one of which involves the use of multiple levels of rank shifted configurations of mathematical Operative processes and participants. The dense texture of mathematics pedagogical discourse arises from the inclusion of these symbolic constructions in the linguistic metadiscourse.' (O'Halloran, 2000, p. 359).

CONCLUSION

Devlin's and O'Halloran's descriptions applies not only to mathematics, but to all domains of knowledge that share the fundamental need to observe, recognize, label, encode, process and communicate distinct regularities. 'For example, *breast cancer* is a disease occurring in a particular part of the body… the two individual features *breast* and *cancer*… would not capture the meaning of the phrase *breast cancer*… which also captures the semantically equivalent expression *neoplasm of the breast*' (Blake & Pratt, 2001, p. 59). Such specialized use of language, focused on disambiguating the meaning of lexical labels – i.e., code words in context within a discipline - has been widely recognized by specialists in terminology, lexicography and communication: 'the absence of ambiguity and the single reference of a term to a concept are essential elements for effective communication' (Cabre, 1998, p. 40)[2].

A lexical label may be a single sign or a sequence of signs in a mono-level sign system namely, words in natural language. Here are a few examples: the words 'spin', 'strangeness' and 'color' are lexical labels of concepts in particle physics where they encode meanings that are very different from their everyday use in English. In musical theory 'ground' is a type of variation form in which a short melodic line occurs repeatedly in the bottom voice. 'Scaffolding' is a lexical label of a concept in learning theory; and 'flying buttress' is a lexical label of a concept in architecture that is unrelated to flying. A lexical label may also be expressions borrowed from another primary sign system (i.e., another language; for example "bulimia nervosa"; "piano nubile"); or signs from a secondary sign system (e.g., CO_2; ♩; $X^{1/3}$); or a combination of several such elements in a multilevel sign system. In addition to natural language, secondary, specialized sign systems are often used in a concept statement for extra clarity and precision (e.g., F# Major); they include visual images; symbols (e.g., mathematical, physical, chemical, biological, etc.). Such specialized use of language was described by Einstein and Infeld (1938): 'science must create its own language, its own concepts, for its own use. Scientific concepts often begin with those used in ordinary language for the affairs of everyday life, but they develop quite differently. They are transformed and lose the ambiguity associated with them in ordinary language, gaining in rigorousness so that they may be applied to scientific thought' (p. 13).

Recently the use of controlled vocabularies became the norm for organizing, searching, and communicating content in virtually all knowledge domains: 'A review of the literature… shows that numerous studies, in various disciplines, have found that a quarter to a third of records returned in a keyword search would be lost without controlled vocabulary. Other writers, though, have continued to suggest that controlled vocabulary be discontinued… this study replicates the search process in the same online catalog, but after the addition of automated enriched metadata such as tables of contents and summaries. The proportion of results that would be lost remains high.' (Gross et. al, 2015).

'The volume of digital data are currently doubling in size every two years... In this environment, indexing languages are a key component of information systems, especially in contexts associated with highly complex, high-quality information, such as professional or academic information. In such cases, they are used both to represent the content of documents and to facilitate access to them. In other words, they are used both to index the documents and to specify users' information needs. Thesauri, taxonomies, ontologies and authority lists are all examples of indexing languages in which the vocabulary is controlled... They are called "controlled vocabularies" because they use sets of descriptors to prevent the ambiguity of natural language. To this end, in these languages each concept is identified with a unique term. An exhaustive compilation of controlled vocabularies can be found at Taxonomy Warehouse. However, in the current Google era, users have grown used to simple search systems, in which they need only enter keywords in a search box to be taken to the information they need. Although these systems have proven to be quite effective, they nevertheless have certain shortcomings. For instance, in scientific literature searches, they can make it difficult for researchers to find the exact information required... One reason for this is because academic databases, and complex information repositories in general, lack the signals, such as link analysis, that Google uses to return web pages. The trend imposed by search engines has rekindled the debate over the usefulness and viability of controlled vocabularies… The debate dates back decades, although it initially focused on the use of controlled vocabularies at libraries. Numerous studies have shown that controlled vocabularies continue to be an essential tool for helping users access information in the aforementioned contexts... As a result, indexing processes based on controlled vocabularies remain necessary in contexts that both make intensive use of information with common features and require effective information retrieval systems. Intranets and subject or institutional repositories are two other clear cases in which the indexing process is effective' (Vállez, Pedraza-Jiménez, & Codina 2015).

REFERENCES

Atran, S., & Medin, D. (2008). *The Native Mind and the Cultural Construction of Nature*. Cambridge, Mass: MIT Press.

Barnbrook, G. (2002). *Defining Language: A Local Grammar of Definition Sentences*. Amsterdam: John Benjamin. doi:10.1075/scl.11

Barnbrook, G., Danielsson, P., & Mahlberg, M. (2005). *Meaningful Texts: The Extraction of Semantic Information from Monolingual and Multilingual Corpora*. London: Continuum.

Bergholz, H., & Tarp, S. (1995). *Manual of Specialised Lexicography*. Amsterdam: Johns Benjamins Publishing.

Blake, C., & Pratt, W. (2001) Better Rules Fewer Features: A Semantic Approach to Selecting Features from Text. In *Proceedings of the Institute of Electrical and Electronics Engineers Data Mining Conference (IEEE-DM)*, p59-66, San Jose, CA. doi:10.1109/ICDM.2001.989501

Bloomfield, L. (1938). Linguistic aspects of science. In O. Neurath, R. Carnap and C. Morris (Eds.), International Encyclopedia of Unified Science, vol. I, nos. 1-5, pp. 215-277.Chicago: University of Chicago Press, 1955.

Cabre, M. T. (1998). *Terminology: Theory, Methods, and Applications*. Amsterdam: Johns Benjamins Publishing.

Carroll, L. (1982). *Alice's Adventures in Wonderland and Through the Looking-Glass and What Alice Found There*. Oxford University Press.

Chemla, K. (2004). *History of Science, History of Text*. Dordrecht, NL: Springer. doi:10.1007/1-4020-2321-9

Crystal, D. (2000). *Language Death*. Cambridge University Press. doi:10.1017/CBO9781139106856

Devlin, K. (1996). *Mathematics: The Science of Patterns*. NY: Scientific American Library.

Einstein, A., & Infeld, L. (1938). *The Evolution of Physics: From Early Concepts to Relativity and Quanta*. NY: Simon and Shuster.

Gorsky, D. P. (1981). *Definition: Logico-Methodological Problems*. Moscow: Progress Publishers.

Gosden, C. (2005). What Do Objects Want? *Journal of Archaeological Method and Theory*, *12*(3), 193–211. doi:10.1007/s10816-005-6928-x

Grishman, R. (2001). Adaptive information extraction and sublanguage analysis. In *Proceedings of the Workshop on Adaptive Text Extraction and Mining at the 17th Joint Conference on Artificial Intelligence*.

Gross, T., Taylor, A. G., & Joudrey, D. N. (2015). Still a Lot to Lose: The Role of Controlled Vocabulary in Keyword Searching. *Cataloging & Classification Quarterly*, *53*(1), 1–39. doi:10.1080/01639374.2014.917447

Harris, Z. (1988). *Language and Information*. Columbia University Press.

Harris, Z., & Mattick, P. (1988). Science sublanguages and the prospect for a global language of science. Annals of the American Academy of Political and Social Science, Vol. 495, Telescience: Scientific Communication in the Information Age, 73-83. Oxford: Pergamon Press.

Harrison, K. D. (2007). *When Languages Die: The Extinction of the World's Languages and the Erosion of Human Knowledge*. Oxford University Press. doi:10.1093/acprof:oso/9780195181920.001.0001

Hurford, J. R. (2007). *The Origins of Meaning*. Oxford University Press.

Johannsen, N., Jessen, M., & Jensen, H. J. (2012). *Excavating the Mind*. Aahrus, Denmark: Aahrus University Press.

Kageura, K. (2002). *The Dynamics of Terminology: A Descriptive Theory of Term Formation and Terminological Growth*. Amsterdam: Johns Benjamins Publishing. doi:10.1075/tlrp.5

Kittredge, R., & Lehrberger, J. (1982). *Sublanguage: Studies of Language in Restricted Semantic Domains*. Berlin: Walter de Gruyter. doi:10.1515/9783110844818

Kittredge, R. I. (1983). Sematic Processing of Texts in Restricted Sublanguages. In N. J. Cercone (Ed.), Computational Linguistics. 45-58.

Macia, E. A., Cervera, A. S., & Ramos, C. R. (2006). *Information Technology in Languages for Specific Purposes*. Springer. doi:10.1007/978-0-387-28624-2

Matthews, A. (1998). *A Diagram of Definition: The Defining of Definition*. Assen, Netherlands: Van Gorcum.

Mayer, F. (2001). Language for Special Purposes: Perspectives for the New Millennium.: Vol. I. *Linguistics and Cognitive Aspects, Knowledge Representation and Computational Linguistics, Terminology, Lexicography and Didactics*. Tubingen: Gunter Narr Verlag.

Miller, J. W. (1980). *The Definition of the Thing with Some Notes on Language*. Norton.

Morley, I., & Renfrew, C. (2010). *The Archeology of Measurement: Comprehending Heaven, Earth and Time in Ancient Societies*. Cambridge University Press. doi:10.1017/CBO9780511760822

Nettle, D., & Romaine, S. (2000). *Vanishing Voices: The Extinction of the World's Languages*. Oxford University Press.

OHalloran, K. L. (2000). Classroom Discourse in Mathematics: A Multisemiotic Analysis. [Elsevier Science Inc.]. *Linguistics and Education*, *10*(3), 359–388. doi:10.1016/S0898-5898(99)00013-3

Olson, D. R. (1994). *The World on Paper: The Conceptual and Cognitive Implications of Writing and Reading*. Cambridge University Press.

Peat, F. D. (1996). *Blackfoot Physics: A Journey into the Native American Universe*. London: Fourth Estate.

Robinson, R. (1950). *Definition*. Oxford at the Clarendon Press.

Sager, J. C. (1990). *A Practical Course in Terminology Processing*. Amsterdam: Johns Benjamins Publishing. doi:10.1075/z.44

Sager, J. C. (1993). *Language Engineering and Translation: Consequences of Automation*. Amsterdam: Johns Benjamins Publishing.

Sager, J. C. (2000). *Essays on Definition*. Amsterdam: Johns Benjamins Publishing. doi:10.1075/tlrp.4

Sager, N. (1986). Sublanguages: Linguistic Phenomenon, Computational Tool. In R. Grishman & R. Kittredge (Eds.), *Analyzing Language in Restricted Domains: Sublanguage Description and Processing* (pp. 1–17).

Vállez, M., Pedraza-Jiménez, R., Codina, L., Blanco, S., & Rovira, C. (2015). Updating controlled vocabularies by analysing query logs. *Online Information Review*, *39*(7), 870–884. doi:10.1108/OIR-06-2015-0180

Wang, X. (2007). *Incommensurability and Cross-Language Communication*. Burlington, VT: Ashgate Publishing.

Wilson, D., & Sperber, D. (2012). *Meaning and Relevance*. Cambridge University Press. doi:10.1017/CBO9781139028370

Yoon, C. K. (2009). *Naming Nature: The Clash between Instinct and Science*. New York: Norton.

ENDNOTES

[1]   We thank Dr. Seamus Ross for calling our attention to this reference.

[2]   While a detailed review of the literature is beyond the scope of the present book, see: Barnbrook, 2002; Barnbrook et al., 2005; Grishman, 2001; Harris, 1988; Harris & Mattick, 1988; Kittredge & Lehrberger, 1982; Sager N., 1986, on sublanguage analysis; Mayer, 2001; Macia et al., 2006, on LSP; Chemla, 2005, and Olson, 1994, on the historical development of the use of text for scientific discourse; Barnbrook, 2002; Gorsky, 1981; Matthews, 1998; Miller, 1980; Robinson, 1950; and Sager J., 2000, on definitions; Cabre, 1998; Kageura, 2002; and Sager J., 1990, on terminology; Bergholz & Tarp, 1995, on lexicography; Sager J., 1993, on translation.

Chapter 3
Concept Parsing
Algorithms (CPA)

ABSTRACT

This chapter describe Concept Parsing Algorithms (CPA), a novel methodology of using text analysis tools for discovery of 'building blocks' of concepts, with semantic searches of the full text of potentially relevant documents in relevant knowledge domains, for lexical labels of concepts in controlled vocabularies. The meaning of lexical label of a super-ordinate concept C' in a sublanguage with controlled vocabulary is encoded in a set that contains three sets of building blocks: Ci (set of co-occurring sub-ordinate concepts); Rj (set of relations); and Lk (set of linguistic elements/descriptors).

INTRODUCTION

In the *Print Age* content was made accessible to library readers through curated paper card catalogues that included meta-tags encoded in Dewey Decimal Classification (DDC), that facilitate reader access to individual documents, namely, books, journals, reports, etc. DDC is a general knowledge organization tool (see: DDC 22 Summaries at oclc.org), where basic classes are organized by disciplines or fields of study. In the *Digital Age,* electronic catalogs provide the same meta-data electronically (see: Markey, 2015). Recent proliferation of digital books allows the inclusion in the functionality of electronic catalog a novel, game-changing feature of *Conceptual Curation* – semantic searches of the full text of potentially relevant documents in relevant knowledge domains

DOI: 10.4018/978-1-5225-2176-1.ch003

for names of concepts in controlled vocabularies. For a given 'super-ordinate' concept of interest, conceptual curation identifies collocated concepts, and reveal the conceptual context of a concept by identifying co-occurrences with other relevant concepts. Such co-occurrence may occur at the level of sentence, paragraph, page, or chapter. In a prescient view of semiotics of concepts, the linguist-semanticist de Beaugrande (1980) described conceptual meaning as embedded in a network of a knowledge domain as 'meaning of a concept is experienced by standing at its control center in a network and looking outward along all of its relational links in that knowledge space' (p. 68). In other words, de Beaugrande's description of 'conceptual meaning' foresaw it as facilitated by conceptual curation.

MAIN FOCUS OF THE CHAPTER

Issues, Controversies, Problems

In the following discussion we define as 'super-ordinate' a concept at the focus of interest, and denote it C'. Equation (3) is a set-theoretic definition of the super-ordinate concept C' in terms of its three building blocks, each containing a specific type of features/descriptors; this equation can be used as a generic format of *Concept Parsing Algorithms (CPA)* that guide the unpacking of C' into its component parts:

$$C' = \{[Ci], [Rj], [Lk]\} \tag{3}$$

The meaning of a lexical label of a super-ordinate concept C' in a sublanguage with controlled vocabulary is encoded in a set that contains three building blocks (Shafrir & Etkind, 2005; 2006); these are the sets:

$[Ci]$ = set of co-occurring sub-ordinate concepts $[C_1, C_2, ..., Cm]$
$[Rj]$ = set of relations $[R_1, R_2, ..., Rn]$
$[Lk]$ = set of linguistic elements (descriptors) $[L_1, L_2, ..., Lp]$

Sets $[Ci]$, $[Rj]$ and $[Lk]$ in Equation (3) can be characterized by the following (non-exhaustive) list of descriptors:
Set $[Ci]$ of Co-occurring Concepts:

1. The set must contain at least two co-occurring concepts (i >= 2; cannot be an empty set)
2. Each concept has a unique lexical label which acts as a proper name; no synonyms are allowed
3. Each concept occurs unconditionally
4. Co-occurring concepts are unranked
5. No metric is available for comparing co-occurring concepts

Set [Rj] of Relations:

- The set may be empty (j =0)
- A relation does not have a unique lexical label and may accept synonyms
- A relation may be between co-occurring concepts, or between co-occurring concepts and the super-ordinal concept
- A relation between two concepts is unconditional
- Relations are unranked
- No metric is available for comparing relations

Set [Lk] of Linguistic Elements:

- The set may not be empty (k >=1)
- Linguistic elements must obey syntactic, morphological, and grammatical rules of the language

SOLUTIONS AND RECOMMENDATIONS

Super-ordinate concepts whose building blocks contain only sub-ordinate concepts, but no relations (i.e., [Rj] is an empty set) are called *containment concepts* (Laurence & Margolis, 1999). Super-ordinate concepts whose building blocks contain both sub-ordinate concepts and relations (i.e., [Rj] is *not* an empty set) are called *inferential concepts* (Shafrir & Etkind, 2005).

Linguistic Parsing

According to Klein (1968/1992[1]) such linguistic parsing and identification of constituent parts are rooted in the transformation from ancient to modern conceptualization of mathematics in the Middle Ages (p. 125). Such linguistic parsing is also reminiscent of Carnap's philosophy of logical positivism, in what he called 'constitutional definition' of concepts (Naess, 1968, p. 26). Carnap (1967) construction theory held that "each scientific statement can in principle be so transformed that it is nothing but a structure statement" (p. 29). According to Carnap, the resultant structure statement explicitly identifies the constituent elements of the concept under consideration. In discussing "the unity of the language of science", Carnap considered 'definition' as an intra-linguistic translation of lexical labels, and showed that concept statements are habitually used to provide comprehensive definitions of concepts in disciplines as different as physics, biology and psychology (Carnap, 1938, pp. 52-60). A similar statement by the physicist Brian Green is quoted by Angier (2007, p. 28): 'In principle, every equation can be expressed in English as a sentence'.

It is noteworthy that the generic parsing procedure outlined above can be applied recursively to each of the co-occurring (sub-ordinate) concepts; the results of such recursive application would be to substitute deeper and deeper levels of sub-ordinate concepts in the definition of a super-ordinate concept. The consequence of such linguistic parsing and substitution of concepts is the concomitant emergence of a detailed concept map of the explored content area (Figure 1). This is a direct consequence of the process of repeated elaborations of the meanings of super-ordinate concepts and their constituent conceptual parts that eventually leads to linguistic representations that contain only words in general language, whose meaning is shared by all competent users of the language - specialists and non-specialists alike. The outcome would therefore be the transformation of a scientific statement in a discipline-specific sublanguage to a statement with equivalent meaning,

Figure 1. Exploration of structure and conceptual meaning of lexical label c': recursive application of CPA reveal deeper levels of building blocks $[c(_{level,i})]$ and $[r(_{level,j})]$

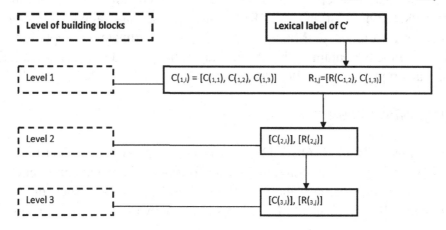

but expressed in general language. We illustrate this process, anticipated by Carnap, with the following example.

Ethnographic research in south-central Bolivia among Quencha-speaking peoples on number values and relations, revealed a highly specialized use of language for the specification of geometrical patterns in weaving. Urton (1997) describes a 'recipe' for weaving a particular design of *Cha'ska* (star) motifs on narrow bands. This design has a unique lexical label - *Chakrupatacha Palmita* (Figure 2) - and Urton illustrates the 'recipe' for this design with detailed lists of weaving sequences presented in three different ways: (1) a 'number grid from picking sequences' of the pattern; (2) a table of 'picking

Figure 2. Weave pattern chakrupatacha palmita of quencha-speaking peoples in south-central bolivia
(Urton, 1997, fig. 4.8; woven by the author)

sequences'; (3) translated into text that describes these picking sequences in regular language (pp. 124-128).

1. The 'number grid from picking sequences':
    '6 - 1/1 - 4 - 6'

This cryptic series of numbers become more explicit in the:

2. 'Picking sequences' description:
    a. '6 white / drop one white and one red / 4 red / 6 white'

Finally, the same line, when presented in

3. Text includes detailed procedural descriptions:
    a. Beginning from the right side of the band, moving to the left, pick up the first 6 white threads; this implies not selecting (i.e., "dropping", or putting down) the colored thread associated with each of these 6 white threads.
    b. Drop or push down the next (i.e., the seventh) white thread, as well as the subsequent red threads.
    c. Pick up the next 4 red threads.
    d. Pick up the following 6 white threads. Now, insert weft between the threads that were picked up and those that were pushed down. Pull the heddle and move on to the picking sequence in line 2.'

These three descriptions of *Chakrupatacha Palmita* can be easily sorted by level of abstraction, with (1) being the most abstract, accessible only to specialists familiar with the sublanguage of weaving these type of patterns. This 'formula' - a sequence of numbers – is made somewhat explicit in (2) *'picking sequences'*; finally, it is (3) that is 'translated' into ordinary language to reveal the meaning of each number in the sequence. As Carnap would expect, this process of recursive substitution of sub-ordinate co-occurring concepts results in a detailed textual description – [a] through [d] in (3) above - accessible to any competent user of the Quencha language.

In *Philosophical Investigations* Wittgenstein (1967, §2) describes such situations as 'language-games', and discuss an example of a pattern consisting of a particular arrangement of 3 X 3 color pieces that contain Red, Green, White and Black squares (§48), shown in Figure (3).

Wittgenstein point out that this arrangement may be described by the sentence:

'R R B G G G R W W'

consisting of the four words "R","G", "W", "B" in the language that correspond to Red, Green, White and Black colors. This sentence describes the meaning of the *lexical label 'Wittgenstein language-game §48'*: 'An example of something corresponding to the name, and without which it would have no meaning, is a paradigm that is used in connexion with the name in the language-game' (Wittgenstein, 1967, §55).

Following Equation (3), CPA representation of this pattern is:

C' = Lexical label of a super-ordinate concept

'Wittgenstein's language game §48'

Figure 3. Pattern of color squares in Wittgenstein's language-game §48

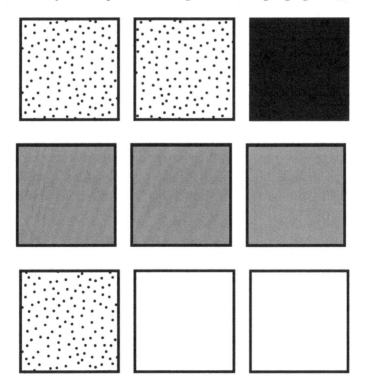

[Ci] = set of co-occurring sub-ordinate concepts

[C_1 = Red, C_2, = Green, C_3 = White, C_4 = Black]

[Rj] = set of relations
[R_1 = to the right of, R_2 = to the left of, R_3 = above, R_4 = below]
[Lk] = set of linguistic elements (descriptors) [L_1, L_2, ...]

These last two examples – 'Chakrupatacha Palmita'; *and* 'Wittgenstein language-game §48' – explicate the relations between a lexical label and its meaning, defined by a detailed description in a language or a sub-language.

Indirect support for the above analysis and Concept Parsing Algorithms (CPA) described by the generic equation (3) comes from review of recent research on the organization and representation of conceptual knowledge in the brain (Mahon & Caramazza, 2007). It reveals disproportionate deficits in brain-damaged patients in naming and in describing objects from different semantic categories (e.g., 'animate living' vs. 'inanimate living'). For example, in response to the lexical label 'Melon' a patient failed to name features of building blocks (sub-ordinate co-occurring concepts and relations) of this concept; however, the same patient, in response to the lexical label 'Lion', generated a detailed list of features of its building blocks (Hillis & Caramazza, 1991).

CONCLUSION

Concept Parsing Algorithms (CPA) is a generic methodology applicable to all knowledge domains, including science; mathematics; social science; humanities; as well as public and private organizations' own digital data bases with the particular organization's own controlled vocabulary (Shafrir & Kenett, 2010).

REFERENCES

Angier, N. (2007). *The Canon*. Boston: Houghton Mifflin.

Carnap, R. (1938). Logical foundations of the unity of science. In O. Neurath, R. Carnap, and C. Morris (Eds.), International Encyclopedia of Unified Science, Vol. I, Nos. 1-5, pp. 42-62. Chicago, Ill: The University of Chicago Press.

Carnap, R. (1967). *The Logical Structure of the World*. Berkeley, Los Angeles: University of California Press.

de Beaugrande, R. (1980). *Text, Discourse, and Process: Toward a Multidisciplinary Science of Texts*. Norwood, New Jersey: ABLEX Publishing.

Hillis, A. E., & Caramazza, A. (1991). Category-specific naming and comprehension impairment: A double dissociation. *Brain, 114*(5), 2081–2094. doi:10.1093/brain/114.5.2081 PMID:1933235

Klein, J. (1968/1992). *Greek Aritmetical Thought and the Origins of Algebra*. New York: Dover Publications.

Mahon, B. Z., & Caramazza, A. (2007). The organization and representation of conceptual knowledge in the brain: Living kinds and artifacts. In E. Margolis & S. Lawrence (Eds.), Creations of the Mind. Oxford University Press.

Markey, K. (2015). *Online Searching: A guide to finding quality information efficiently and effectively*. Rowman & Littlefield.

Naess, A. (1968). *Four Modern Philosophers: Carnap; Wittgenstein; Heidegger; Sartre*. Chicago: University of Chicago Press.

Shafrir, U., & Etkind, M. (2005). *Concept Parsing Algorithms: Mapping the Conceptual Content of Disciplines. Version 11.0 (January, 2005)*. Toronto: PARCEP.

Shafrir, U., & Etkind, M. (2006). eLearning for depth in the semantic web. *British Journal of Educational Technology, 37*(3), 425–444. doi:10.1111/j.1467-8535.2006.00614.x

Shafrir, U., & Kenett, R. S. (2010). Conceptual thinking and metrology concepts. [Springer.]. *Accreditation and Quality Assurance*, *15*(10), 585–590. doi:10.1007/s00769-010-0669-6

Urton, G. (1997). *The Social Life of Numbers: A Quenchua Ontology of Numbers and Philosophy of Arithmetic*. Austin: University of Texas Press.

Wittgenstein, L. (1967). *Philosophical Investigations* (2nd ed.). (G. E. M. Anscombe, Trans.). Oxford: Basil Blackwell.

ENDNOTE

[1]   We thank Dr. Geoffrey Bowker for calling our attention to this reference.

Chapter 4
Evolving Concepts

ABSTRACT

This chapter describe the evolution of concepts with Concept Parsing Algorithms (CPA) that captures both the conceptual content and the conceptual structure of a context within a domain of knowledge, and results in a comprehensive, schematic description of important concepts at the time of analysis. Online availability of digital books, journals, comprehensive datasets, etc., lead to the evolution of research methods that expand the potential of CPA for exploring co-occurrence of concepts beyond the literature of a particular area in a knowledge domain, that may also include 'neighbouring' areas in the knowledge domain. It supports the evolution of the novel research methodology Literature-Based Discovery (LBD).

INTRODUCTION

Systematic application of CPA in context within a discipline generates a concept map that reveals hierarchical and lateral links between concepts and their relations. CPA document hierarchical links between super-ordinate and sub-ordinate co-occurring concepts (set $[C_i]$). CPA also document lateral links that reveal relations between the co-occurring concepts (these concepts may also appear elsewhere in the concept map as super-ordinate concepts or as sub-ordinate concepts of other super-ordinate concepts). Systematic application

DOI: 10.4018/978-1-5225-2176-1.ch004

of CPA captures both the conceptual content and the conceptual structure of a context within a domain of knowledge, and results in a comprehensive, schematic description of its important concepts at the time of analysis.

MAIN FOCUS OF THE CHAPTER

Issues, Controversies, Problems

It is important to remember that, often, conceptual content and the conceptual structure of a context within a domain of knowledge undergoes changes. The diachronic nature of concept maps in many disciplines is one outcome of a feedback-driven process that reflects the continuous scientific scrutiny and testing-against-reality of patterns in the data, new and old alike, and that inevitably results in discovery of new super-ordinate concepts. Recent research documented improvement in class discussions and learning outcomes in high school physics courses taught by physics teachers who took 'Conceptual History of Physics' course as part of their Professional Development activities (Garik et al., 2015).

Concept maps are therefore in a permanent state of flux due to the continuing, incremental development of knowledge in particular contexts within a discipline: 'It is important to distinguish between the concept and its stages. Between one expansion and the next we have one stage of the concept, and after the expansion we have another stage of the same concept' (Buzaglo, 2002; p. 73).

A recent example is the assembly of the International Astronomical Union (IAU), when it approved on August 24, 2006, by an overwhelming majority, resolutions that re-defined the meaning of the lexical label of the concept *"planet"*. In a preamble, IAU explained the reason for these controversial decisions:

'Contemporary observations are changing our understanding of planetary systems, and it is important that our nomenclature for objects reflect our current understanding. This applies, in particular, to the designation 'planets'. The word 'planet' originally described 'wanderers' that were known only as moving lights in the sky. Recent discoveries lead us to create a new definition, which we can make using currently available scientific information' (https://www.iau.org/news/pressreleases/detail/iau0603/).

IAU resolutions include the following new definitions of "planet".

RESOLUTIONS

Resolution 5A is the principal definition for the IAU usage of "planet" and related terms.

Resolution 6A creates for IAU usage a new class of objects, for which Pluto is the prototype. The IAU will set up a process to name these objects.

RESOLUTION 5A

The IAU therefore resolves that planets and other bodies in our Solar System, except satellites, be defined into three distinct categories in the following way:

1. A "planet"[1] is a celestial body that (a) is in orbit around the Sun, (b) has sufficient mass for its self-gravity to overcome rigid body forces so that it assumes a hydrostatic equilibrium (nearly round) shape, and (c) has cleared the neighbourhood around its orbit.
2. A "dwarf planet" is a celestial body that (a) is in orbit around the Sun, (b) has sufficient mass for its self-gravity to overcome rigid body forces so that it assumes a hydrostatic equilibrium (nearly round) shape[2], (c) has not cleared the neighbourhood around its orbit, and (d) is not a satellite.
3. All other objects[3], except satellites, orbiting the Sun shall be referred to collectively as "Small Solar-System Bodies".

IAU Resolution: Pluto

RESOLUTION 6A

The IAU further resolves:

Pluto is a "dwarf planet" by the above definition and is recognized as the prototype of a new category of trans-Neptunian objects.'[1]

The validity of the concept 'dwarf planet' was reaffirmed and enhanced recently: 'Astronomers have discovered another dwarf planet in the Kuiper Belt, the ring of icy objects beyond Neptune. But this newfound world, dubbed 2015 RR245, is much more distant than Pluto, orbiting the sun once every

700 Earth years' (http://www.space.com/33387-dwarf-planet-discovery-2015-rr245.html).

SOLUTIONS AND RECOMMENDATIONS

This highlights the time-dependent, diachronic nature of CPA-guided concept mapping, the conceptual evolution of individual disciplines by identifying building blocks of historical conceptualizations that did not pass the test of time. For example, 'aether' was a lexical label of a concept in physics with building blocks that were undergoing revision, as a result of the conceptual revolution following Einstein's publication of the theory of special relativity in 1905. The astrophysicist Sir Arthur Eddington wrote the following words in 1928: "Thirty years ago there was much debate over the question of aether-drag – whether the earth moving round the sun drags the aether with it… it was widely believed that aether was a kind of matter, having properties such as mass, rigidity, motion, like ordinary matter… Nowadays it is agreed that aether is not a kind of matter… we cannot say whether the aether now in this room is flowing out through the north wall or the south wall. The question would have a meaning for a material ocean, but there is no reason to expect it to have a meaning for the non-material ocean of aether" (Eddington, 1958; pp. 3 and 31-32). Soon after, it became clear that 'aether' was not a viable physical concept, namely, not an invariant - pattern in the physical data - and it went the way of the phlogiston (see: https://www.britannica.com/science/phlogiston).

Unlike 'aether', the concept 'Day' fared much better in the history of geophysics. It is mentioned in an early 'physics text' – the Bible - in the first verses of the first chapter of The Book of Genesis (Revised Standard Version; http://www.fordham.edu/HALSALL/ANCIENT/genesis-rsv.html):

'3 And God said, 'Let there be light'; and there was light.
4 And God saw that the light was good; and God separated the light from
    the darkness.
5 God called the light Day, and the darkness he called Night. And there was
    evening and there was morning, one day.'

'Light' is a direct sensory input, and sentence (3) does not provide any clues for the existence of building blocks. However, (4) and (5) provide details of features defining the lexical label

C' = Day

as an emergent super-ordinate concept with building blocks [Ci] and [Rj], with the following sets of features:

[Ci] = [light, night, darkness]
[Rj] = [separate, morning, evening]

While bible researchers do not agree on the date in which these words where first written, most seem to believe that biblical text reflects an historical-cultural oral tradition dating back to the first half of the second millennium BC, and that it was probably inscribed into text in the first half on the first millennium BC (Schniedewind, 2004). The basic physical concept 'Day' as defined by Genesis still holds today, although it has obviously been refined through the continuous accumulation of observations of periodical changes in the time interval between morning and evening.

Physicists generally agree that evolving conceptualizations in physics reflect the evolving state of our knowledge of the physical world, and new research findings prompt subsequent re-conceptualizations. This state of affairs should not be taken for granted in other disciplines. For example, the state of knowledge of medical specialists at any given time is not the only important variable in medical science; there is evidence that the very nature of a particular medical phenomenon under investigation may be constantly changing, with concomitant changes in evolving conceptualizations. For example Bowker & Star (1999, p. 168) state that 'the disease is constantly in motion' and label Tuberculosis 'a moving target'. They describe the temporal variability of HIV across individuals in these words: 'HIV, for example, mutates rapidly in the individual sufferer, so that no two people suffer from the same disease, nor may the disease be identical with itself over time even within a person' (p. 90).

Literature-Based Discovery (LBD)

Online availability of digital books, journals, comprehensive datasets, etc., lead to the evolution of research methods that expand the potential of Concept Parsing Algorithms (CPA) for exploring co-occurrence of concepts beyond the literature of a particular area in a knowledge domain, that may also include 'neighbouring' areas in the knowledge domain. It supports the evolution of a novel research methodology Literature-Based Discovery (LBD), (see: Yakub et al., 2017; Cameron et al., 2015).

Here is an example of using CPA to document Swanson's (1988) research of *Raynaud's syndrome*.

Based on searching for collocated concepts from relevant medical literature in MEDLINE, Swanson encoded the meaning of

C' = *'Raynaud's syndrome'*

in terms of two levels of building blocks

Level 1 $C_{(1,i)}$ = [circulatory, disorder, ...]

$R_{1,j}$ = [periphery, ...]
Level 2 $C_{(2,i)}$ = [blood viscosity, platelet aggregability, vascular reactivity, ...]
$R_{(2,j)}$ = [high, ...]

In addition, and independently of the above, there existed at the time another collection of medical literature in another context within MEDLINE, in which *eicosapentaenoic acid* (the active ingredient in fish-oil) was shown to cause reduction in blood viscosity, platelet aggregability, and vascular reactivity.

Figure 1. Swanson's discovery of treatment for Raynaud's syndrome by exploring deeper building blocks

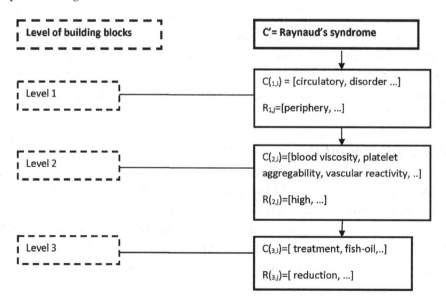

Putting together search results in these two different medical literatures, Swanson's research resulted in the formulation of a new hypothesis, namely, treatment of Raynaud's syndrome with eicosapentaenoic acid (Figure 1):

Level 3 $C_{(3,i)}$ = [treatment, fish-oil, …]
$R_{(3,j)}$ = [reduction, …]

This hypothesis was confirmed in independent medical research (Chang et al., 1988). In a follow-up study, Swanson discovered that "magnesium deficiency… led to certain physiological effects… that, in a different context, were associated with migraine" (Swanson, 1997, p. 185).

CONCLUSION

Subsequent research documented additional examples of deeper roots of building blocks of super-ordinate concepts in medicine, bio-warfare, and genetics (Swanson, Smalheiser, & Torvik, 2006; see also van der Eijk et al., 2004; Wren et al., 2004).

LBD open new cross-disciplinary co-citation links that span the boundaries of previously disconnected research areas, may point to their mutual relevance (Yakub et al., 2017), and statistical verification with Diagnostic Classification Models (DCMs; Rupp et al., 2010).

This research provide support for Concept Parsing Algorithms (CPA) as a valid and productive methodology for enhancing learning and research outcomes with Literature-Based Discovery (LBD).

REFERENCES

Bowker, G. C., & Star, S. L. (1999). *Sorting Things Out: Classification and Its Consequences*. Cambridge, MA: MIT Press.

Buzaglo, M. (2002). *The logic of concept expansion*. Cambridge University Press.

Cameron, D., Kavuluru, R., Rindflesch, T. C., Sheth, A. P., Krishnaprasad Thirunarayan, K., & Bodenreider, O. (2015). Context-driven automatic subgraph creation for literature-based discovery. *Journal of Biomedical Informatics*, *54*, 141–157. doi:10.1016/j.jbi.2015.01.014 PMID:25661592

Chang, B. B., DiGiacomo, R., Kremer, J., Kay, C., & Shah, D. M. (1988). Effects of fish oil fatty acid ingestion in patients with Raynoud's syndrome. Surgica. *Forum*, *39*, 324–326.

Eddington, A. (1958). *The Nature of the Physical World*. Ann Arbor: The University of Michigan Press.

Garik, P., Garbayo, L., Benetro-Dupin, Y., Winrich, C., Duffy, A., Gross, N., & Jariwala, M. (2015). Teaching the Conceptual History of Physics to Physics Teachers. *Science and Education*, *24*(4), 387–408. doi:10.1007/s11191-014-9731-9

Rupp, A. A., Templin, J., & Henson, R. A. (2010). *Diagnostic Measurement: Theory, Methods, and Applications*. New York: Guildford Press.

Schniedewind, W. M. (2004). *How the Bible Became a Book: The Textualization of Ancient Israel*. Cambridge University Press. doi:10.1017/CBO9780511499135

Swanson, D. R. (1988). Migraine and magnesium: Eleven neglected connections. *Perspectives in Biology and Medicine*, *31*(4), 526–557. doi:10.1353/pbm.1988.0009 PMID:3075738

Swanson, D. R., & Smalheiser, N. R. (1997). An interactive system for finding complementary literatures: A stimulus to scientific discovery. *Artificial Intelligence*, *91*(2), 183–203. doi:10.1016/S0004-3702(97)00008-8

Swanson, D. R., Smalheiser, N. R., & Torvik, V. I. (2006). Ranking indirect connections in Literature-Based Discovery: The role of Medical Subject Headings. *Journal of the American Society for Information Science and Technology*, *57*(11), 1427–1439. doi:10.1002/asi.20438

van der Eijk, C. C., van Mulligen, E. M., Kors, J. A., Mons, B., & van den Berg, J. (2004). Constructing an associative concept space for Literature-Based Discovery. *Journal of the American Society for Information Science and Technology*, *55*(5), 436–444. doi:10.1002/asi.10392

Wren, J. D., Bekeredjian, R., Stewart, J. A., Shohet, R. V., & Garner, H. R. (2004). Knowledge discovery by automated identification and ranking of implicit relationships. *Bioinformatics (Oxford, England)*, *20*(3), 389–398. doi:10.1093/bioinformatics/btg421 PMID:14960466

Yakub, S., Eugene, S., & Sylvester, O. O. (2017). Learning the heterogeneous bibliographic information network for literature-based discovery. *Knowledge-Based Systems*, *115*, 66–79. doi:10.1016/j.knosys.2016.10.015

ENDNOTES

[1] The eight planets are: Mercury, Venus, Earth, Mars, Jupiter, Saturn, Uranus, and Neptune.

[2] An IAU process will be established to assign borderline objects into either dwarf planet or other categories.

[3] These currently include most of the Solar System asteroids, most Trans-Neptunian Objects (TNOs), comets, and other small bodies.

Chapter 5
Meaning Equivalence (ME), Boundary of Meaning (BoM), and Granulary of Meaning (GoM)

ABSTRACT

This chapter describe Meaning Equivalence (ME), Boundary of Meaning (BoM), and Granularity of Meaning (GoM). Meaning Equivalence (ME) is a polymorphous - one-to-many - transformation of meaning that signifies the ability to transcode equivalence-of-meaning through multiple representations within and across sign systems, and multiple definitions of a concept in multiple sign systems. Boundary of Meaning (BoM) is the boundary between two mutually exclusive semantic spaces in the sublanguage: (i) semantic space that contains only representations that do share equivalence-of-meaning with the Target Statement (TS); and (ii) semantic space that contains only representations that do not share equivalence-of-meaning with the TS. Granularity of Meaning (GoM) is the deepest level in which lexical label of a co-occurring subordinate concept appears in the Target Statement. It is therefore a measure of the 'depth of exploration' of building blocks of a super-ordinate concept in TS. Boundary of Meaning (BoM) and Granularity of Meaning (GoM) are concepts in Pedagogy for Conceptual Thinking, a novel teaching and learning methodology in the digital age (Etkind, Kenett & Shafrir, 2016). These constructs describe important aspects of learning outcomes.

DOI: 10.4018/978-1-5225-2176-1.ch005

INTRODUCTION

In many situations in daily life we feel the need to express the same meaning by repeating a discourse. This need seems to be non-specific to a particular content, and applies equally to different types of discourse: descriptive; abstract; narrative; and expository. For example, we repeat a narrative discourse when we "tell the same story again". We sometime repeat an expository discourse when, for example, we give a "repeat performance" of a lecture on a specific topic to different sections of a class; or when we have to reconstruct a lost paragraph that has not been saved in time to avoid the calamity of a computer crash. On other occasions, we find it spontaneously convenient to repeat a sentence during a conversation that re-defines a complex conceptual situation. What is the meaning of "repeat" in such circumstances? Does it mean that the second (third, fourth, etc.) repetition is identical – equal in all details – to the first discourse? As is obvious to any competent language user, what we mean by "repeat performance" is not the verbatim quotation of the original discourse, but rather its re-representation: the re-construction and re-transmission of meaning.

While we may often feel that in subsequent representations we expressed 'the same' meaning as in the original discourse, it is easy to verify that, in fact, while conserving the meaning encoded in the original discourse, in subsequent representations we expressed this meaning in different ways. We accomplish this by paraphrasing - putting things 'in other words'; by choice of metaphor; and by changing emphasis, point-of-view, discourse style, etc. Thus the original representation looks (or sounds) different from the second representation of the meaning; which looks/sounds still different from a third representation; etc.

MAIN FOCUS OF THE CHAPTER

Issues, Controversies, Problems

The term *meaning equivalence* (ME) designates this commonality of meaning, the meaning preserved across several such representations. Meaning equivalence is a polymorphous - one-to-many - transformation of meaning; it signifies the ability to transcode equivalence-of-meaning through multiple representations within and across sign systems (Shafrir, 2012; Sigel, 1954; 1993; 2012).

This abstract formulation of the construct of equivalence-of-meaning masks a reality that is implicitly familiar to any language user, namely, the ability to express meaning effortlessly in a multitude of ways. This reality rests on a solid foundation, revealed upon reflection by any keen observer: Any specific meaning, in any discipline, may be represented in a multitude of ways in at least one sign system; often, and in many disciplines, a specific meaning may be represented in a many ways in several sign systems.

The physicist Richard Feynman viewed the construction of multiple representations of mathematical and physical concepts as an important tool in the arsenal of a theoretical physicist's quest to uncover regularities in the universe. This view is shared by other physicists, as well as by scientists in other domains of knowledge (John-Steiner, 1987, p. 184). Feynman was fond of testing his students' depth of comprehension by asking them to paraphrase his descriptions of conceptual physical situations in their own words.

Paraphrase plays an important role not only in communication *within* a community-of-shared-sublanguage such as physics; paraphrase may also play another important role in *communication between specialists and non-specialists*. For example, doctors and other medical professionals regularly face the challenge of constructing representations of conceptually complex medical situations in 'lay language' when communicating with patients. In these situations, prior to signing Informed Consent forms, the lexical labels of concepts in highly abbreviated and abstract diagnosis and treatment plans must be discussed with patients and families using ordinary language (Biron-Shental, et al., 2016). Following EU legislation in 1993, it became a legal requirement to include a Patient Package Insert (PPI)[1] in all medical product packages that is 'easy to read and written in a way which is unambiguous and understandable to the consumer' (Askehave & Zethsen, 2001). These 'lay paraphrases' are the outcomes of intra-linguistic, inter-generic translations in which the source text is a technical document written in a sublanguage, and includes controlled medical vocabulary. However, efforts to avoid the use of such vocabulary sometime lead to ambiguity and confusion by prompting the evolution of folkloristic expressions commonly used to describe medical phenomena in loosely defined 'popular terms' such as: 'Barber's itch'; 'Housewife's dermatitis'; 'Jeep disease'; 'Poker spine'; 'Rum fits'; and 'War neurosis' (Bowker & Star, 1999, pp. 91-94).

Multiple Definitions of a Concept

Lexical label of a concept may be defined in different ways by different sets of building blocks. For example, a super-ordinate concept C' may be defined by two different sets of building blocks, CPA (1) and CPA (2), each containing different sets of co-occurring sub-ordinate concepts, relations, and linguistic descriptors. A simple example is the three definitions of *'circle'* as (i) a geometric place; as well as in two different co-ordinate systems, (ii) Cartesian; and (iii) polar. Following Carnap's rationale, Equation (3) may be applied recursively by substituting in each of the two definitions explicit concept descriptions for their lexical labels. This procedure produce a series of paraphrases. These three definitions of 'circle' will be shown to be equivalent in meaning if 3 chains of recursive reductions. One for the definition of 'circle' as a 'geometric place'; one for the definition of 'circle' in Cartesian coordinates; the third for polar coordinates; will eventually produce three linguistic descriptions of 'circle' that are judged by a majority of general language users to mean the same thing.

Feynman was convinced that, although multiple representations are just reformulations and repetitions of existing knowledge of a known physical phenomenon, it is impossible to know, in advance, which of the representations prove crucial in bridging the way to the construction of new knowledge. In his 1965 Nobel lecture Feynman posited multiplicity of representations as a key aspect of scientific thinking when trying to move from the known to the unknown: "I think the problem is not to find the best or most efficient method to proceed to a discovery, but to find any method at all. Physical reasoning does help some people to generate suggestions as to how the unknown may be related to the known. Theories of the known, which are described by different physical ideas may be equivalent in all their predictions and are hence scientifically indistinguishable. However, they are not psychologically identical when trying to move from that base into the unknown. For different views suggest different kinds of modifications which might be made... I, therefore, think that a good theoretical physicist might find it useful to have a wide range of physical viewpoints and mathematical expressions of the same theory... available to him" (Feynman, 1966, p. 708).

In his lectures to freshmen physics students at California Institute of Technology, Feynman (1963) proved that Kepler's first law which states that all planets move around the sun in elliptical orbits is equivalent to the physical law stating that light rays generated at one of the foci of a reflective ellipse converge at the other focus of the ellipse. In the terminology of CPA developed above, Feynman claimed that Kepler's first law may be defined by two different parsing algorithms, CPA (1) and CPA (2), where:

$$Kepler's\ First\ Law = \begin{cases} CPA\ (1) &= \{[C_{1,i}],\ [R_{1,j}],\ [L_{1,k}]\} \\ CPA\ (2) &= \{[C_{2,i}],\ [R_{2,j}],\ [L_{2,k}]\} \end{cases} \tag{4}$$

Feynman demonstrated the equivalence of these different definitions by leading his students through a series of steps of mathematical-physical reasoning. It started at the upper definition, where the three sets $\{[C_{1,i}],\ [R_{1,j}],$ $[L_{1,k}]\}$ define an elliptical orbit. It then ended at the lower definition where the three sets $\{[C_{2,i}],\ [R_{2,j}],\ [L_{2,k}]\}$ define the physical situation in which light rays are emitted at one focus, reflected by the ellipse, and then converge at the other focus of the ellipse. This method of establishing meaning equivalence of two different expressions that encode the same underlying concept, by constructing intermediate steps and demonstrating that equivalence of meaning is maintained between each two consecutive steps, is often used in the construction of complex mathematical proofs.

It seems that the ideas of multiplicity of equivalent representations of physical laws and the nature of the linguistic reasoning paths connecting them were often on Feynman's mind. Keeping his belief that 'we must always keep all the alternative ways of looking at a thing' Feynman (1965, p. 54) demonstrated to his audience, in the Messenger Lectures, how to move from a geometric description of Newton's laws through language to an algebraic description of these laws. He demonstrated that Newton's Law of Gravitation may be represented (and therefore interpreted) in 3 different ways: as action-at-a-distance; as a field; and by constructing energy integrals of alternative paths of motion of a mass (pp. 40-55). Feynman concluded: "I always find that mysterious, and I do not understand the reason why it is that the correct laws of physics seem to be expressible in such a tremendous variety of ways. They seem to be able to get through several wickets at the same time" (p. 55).

SOLUTIONS AND RECOMMENDATIONS

Viewed within the framework of CPA, Feynman's comment on multiple definitions of concepts reflects the puzzling situation where a lexical label of an important super-ordinate concept in physics – 'gravitational force' – is defined in three different ways, each with its own building blocks - sets of co-occurring sub-ordinate concepts and relations.

Figure 1 illustrates the relations between a lexical label of a concept and two types of relevant statements:

- **Concept Statement (CS):** Comprehensive definition of the concept that specify all features of its building blocks (Teubert, 2005, p. 99)
- **Target Statement (TS):** Describe a particular conceptual situation/ context in a given Concept Statement

In Figure 1 the meaning of the lexical label of the concept C' is defined by three different Concept Statements: CS(1); CS(2); and CS(3). Each of these concept statements anchors several Target Statements TS(i,j), each a different representation of a conceptual situation involving CS(i). For example, in Figure 1, the five Target Statements TS(2,1); TS(2,2); TS(2,3); TS(2,4); and TS(2,5) are associated with CS(2).

CS(2) may have the following building blocks:

$[C_i]$ = set of sub-ordinate co-occurring concepts $[C_1, C_2, C_3, C_4]$
$[R_j]$ = set of relations $[R_1, R_2, R_3]$, where R_1 is a relationship between C_1 and C_2; R_2 is a relation between C' and C_3; and R_3 is a relation between C_3 and C_4

Figure 1. Lexical label of a concept; multiple concept statements cs (i); and target statements ts (i,j)

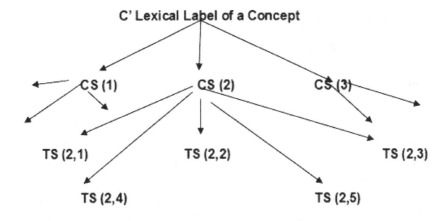

Then:

- TS(2,1) may be a target statement that describes a conceptual situation involving C_1, C_2, C_4, and R_1
- TS(2,2) may be a target statement that describes a conceptual situation involving C', C_2, C_3, and R_2
- TS(2,3) may be still another target statement that describes a conceptual situation involving certain features of building blocks of C_2 e.g., co-occurring sub-ordinate concepts of C_2; as well as sub-ordinate concept C_1, and relation R_3

CONCLUSION

Feynman's comment on multiple definitions of concepts also hints at an important, practical issue of constructing and recognizing multiple representations of a particular conceptual situation that share equivalence-of-meaning. Often, a Target Statement (TS) that encodes a particular conceptual situation has to be compared to other, thematically relevant statements, then making a decision regarding whether they share equivalence-of-meaning. In such situations, one may ask if another thematically relevant statement is located within the Boundary of Meaning (BoM) of a particular Target Statement.

The construct 'Boundary of Meaning' (BoM) may be formulated as follows: Given a community of specialists that share a sublanguage, and a Target Statement that encodes a particular conceptual situation; then BoM is the boundary between two *mutually exclusive semantic spaces* in the sublanguage:

- A semantic space that contains only representations that *do share equivalence-of-meaning* with the Target Statement.
- A semantic space that contains only representations that *do not share equivalence-of-meaning* with the Target Statement.

A practical way to demarcate BoM for a particular Target Statement is to sort thematically relevant statements according to two independent sorting criteria: 'Surface Similarity (SS)' with the Target Statement (TS) and 'Meaning Equivalence (ME)' with TS. By 'Surface Similarity' we mean statements with same/similar words appearing in the same/similar order as in the Target Statement; and by 'Meaning Equivalence' we mean that a majority of specialists that share a sublanguage with controlled vocabulary would agree that the meaning of the statement being sorted is equivalent to the meaning of the Target Statement (Shafrir, 2012). In Figure 2,

- Statements in quadrant Q1 are *similar in appearance* to the target and also *share equivalence-of-meaning* with the target.
- Statements in quadrant Q2 are *not similar in appearance* to the target but *do share equivalence-of-meaning* with it.
- Statements in quadrant Q3 are *similar in appearance* to the target, but *do not share equivalence-of-meaning* with it.
- Statements in quadrant Q4, although thematically related to the target statement, are *not similar in appearance* to the target and *do not share equivalence-of-meaning* with it.

Statements in quadrants Q1 and Q2 share Meaning Equivalence with TS, and therefore are *within BoM*; statements in quadrants Q3 and Q4 do not share Meaning Equivalence with TS, and are *outside BoM*. Therefore, *TS; Q1; and Q2 statements reside within the BoM of TS; Q3; and Q4 statements reside outside of BoM of TS* (Figure 3).

Figure 2. Defining Boundary-of-Meaning (BoM) for a given Target Statement (TS): Surface Similarity (SS) and Meaning Equivalence (ME)

TARGET STATEMENT (TS)

Surface similarity [SS]

	Yes	No	
Q1	SS Yes ME Yes	SS No ME Yes	**Q2**
Q3	SS Yes ME No	SS No ME No	**Q4**

Meaning equivalence [ME] — Yes / No

Figure 3. Boundary-of-Meaning (BoM) for a given Target Statement (TS)

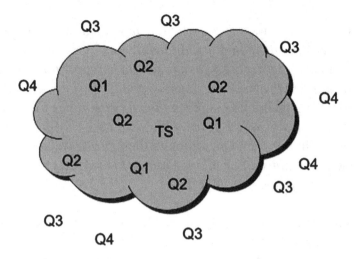

Granularity of Meaning (GoM) is the deepest level in which a lexical label of a co-occurring subordinate concept appears in the Target Statement. GoM is therefore a measure of the 'depth of exploration' of building blocks of a super-ordinate concept in TS. Boundary of Meaning (BoM) and Granularity of Meaning (GoM) are novel concepts in Pedagogy for Conceptual Thinking, a teaching/learning methodology in the digital age. They describe conceptual content, and measure important aspects of learning outcomes (Etkind, Kenett & Shafrir, 2016).

REFERENCES

Askehave, I., & Zethsen, K. K. (2001). Inter-Generic and Inter-linguistic Translation of Patient Package Inserts. In F. Mayer (Ed.), *Languages for Special Purposes: Perspectives for the New Millennium* (Vol. 1, pp. 882–887). Tubingen: Gunter Narr Verlag.

Biron-Shental, T., Kenett, R. S., Shafrir, U., Rosen, H., Garg, S., Farine, D., & Fishman, A. (2016). Evidence Based Informed Consent for Caesarean Section Using MERLO - Meaning Equivalence Reusable Learning Objects. *British Journal of Education, Society & Behavioural Science 17*(2), 1-10.

Bowker, G. C., & Star, S. L. (1999). *Sorting Things Out: Classification and Its Consequences*. Cambridge, MA: MIT Press.

Etkind, M., Kenett, R. S., & Shafrir, U. (2016). Learning in the Digital Age with Meaning Equivalence Reusable Learning Objects (MERLO). In Railean, E., Walker, G., Elçi, A., & Jackson, L. (Eds.), *Handbook of Research on Applied Learning Theory and Design in Modern Education,* pp. 310-333. Hershey, PA: IGI Global.

Feynman, R. (1963). *Feynman's Lectures on Physics*. New York: Addison-Wesley.

Feynman, R. (1965). *The Character of Physical Law*. MIT Press.

Feynman, R. (1966). The development of space-time view of quantum field theory. [Nobel Lecture.]. *Science, 153*(3737), 699–708. doi:10.1126/science.153.3737.699 PMID:17791121

John-Steiner, V. (1987). *Notebooks of the Mind: Explorations of Thinking*. NY: Harper & Row.

Shafrir, U. (2012). Representational competence. In I. E. Sigel (Ed.), *The Development of Mental Representation: Theory and Applications.* (pp. 371-389). Mahwah, NJ: Lawrence Erlbaum Publishers.

Sigel, I. E. (1954). The dominance of meaning. *The Journal of Genetic Psychology, 85*(2), 201–207. doi:10.1080/00221325.1954.10532876 PMID:13221783

Sigel, I. E. (1993). The centrality of a distancing model for the development of representational competence. In R. R. Cocking & K. A. Renninger (Eds.), *The development and meaning of psychological distance* (pp. 141–158).

Sigel, I. E. (2012). Approaches to representation as a psychological construct: a treatise in diversity. In I.E. Sigel (Ed.), *Development of mental representation,* (pp. 3-12). NJ: Lawrence Erlbaum Associates, Inc.

Teubert, W. (2005). Language as an Economic Factor: The Importance of Terminology. In G. Barnbrook, P. Danielsson, & M. Mahlberg (Eds.), *Meaningful Texts: The Extraction of Semantic Information from Monolingual and Multilingual Corpora*. London: Continuum.

ENDNOTE

[1]   We thank Dr. David Boyd for making us aware of PPI.

Chapter 6
Interactive Concept Discovery (INCOD)

ABSTRACT

This chapter describe systematic exploration of important concepts in digital libraries with Key Word in Context (KWIC) semantic search that allow learners to explore specific conceptual situations by searching lexical label of a concept. Comprehensive record of a learner's sequence of searches allows for a detailed reconstruction of the learning episodes generated by Interactive Concept Discovery (InCoD) over time. It reveals the learner's consistency of 'drilling-down' for discovering deeper building blocks of the particular concept, and the temporal evolution of learning outcomes.

INTRODUCTION

Concept Parsing Algorithms (CPA) plays important role in learning and research in the digital age. In addition to traditional reading of a chapter in the course textbook, learners gain understanding of course material by engaging in Interactive Concept Discovery (InCoD), systematic exploration of important concepts in digital libraries. This is a novel Key Word in Context (KWIC) semantic search that allow learners to explore specific conceptual situations by searching lexical label of a concept; to discover concepts and their relations within particular knowledge domains; and to develop deep understanding of real and hypothetical conceptual situations under consideration (Figure 1).

DOI: 10.4018/978-1-5225-2176-1.ch006

Figure 1. Interactive Concept Discovery (InCoD)

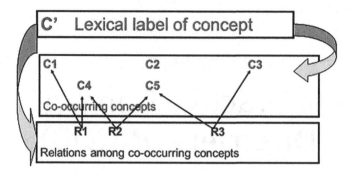

Interactive Concept Discovery (InCoD)

The traditional 'reading list for a course' has been replaced in the digital age by a Knowledge Repository (KR) that contain comprehensive collection of all relevant digital documents (books; journals; technical reports; databased; image-bases). Interactive Concept Discovery with KWIC semantic searches offer learners opportunities to discover a document's *Conceptual Footprint*, by marking all the locations in the document where relevant concepts are mentioned. As well as to compare discussions of specific concepts in different documents written by different authors. The reader is expected to choose several such discussions for comparison and annotation; to construct *Learner Individual Index* of names of concepts and their relations; and drill for deeper roots of building blocks of the concept under scrutiny. Interactive Concept Discovery facilitate the identification of hierarchical and lateral links in, and analysis of, conceptual structure in the course Knowledge Repository. The learner begins by conducting *concordance*, namely, semantic search of Key Word In Context (KWIC) of a Super-Ordinate concept (C'), and evaluating the consistency of appearance of co-occurring concepts and their relations across different documents found to contain (C') lexical label. In each successive iteration, the learner can read/save found documents online; mark/save lexical labels and candidate features of building blocks; annotate and evaluate the degree of relevance of a particular found document to the specific conceptual content under consideration; and construct alternative graphical representations of links between concepts and their building blocks. A comprehensive record of a learner's sequence of iterations allows for a detailed reconstruction of the learning episodes generated by InCoD over time. It reveals the learner's consistency of 'drilling-down' for discovering deeper building blocks of the particular concept, and the temporal evolution of outcomes of the learning sequence. This digital record is an authentic, evidence-based demonstration of mastery of knowledge that can be used as a springboard for a follow-up class and chat room discussions, and provide a credible record to an individual's learning process and enhanced learning outcomes.

MAIN FOCUS OF THE CHAPTER

Issues, Controversies, Problems

Concordance and Co-Occurrence

Figure 2 shows Concordance of the super-ordinate concept (headword) *'colour'* within & across documents in a Knowledge Repository that contain a comprehensive collection of digital documents relevant to the super-ordinal concept *'Chromodynamics'* (physics/elementary particles). This is an initial step in Interactive Concept Discovery (InCoD), to be followed by further semantic searches that explore relations among co-occurring concepts, and deeper layers of co-occurring concepts (Figure 1).

We notice that left of the column of HEADWORD there are 2 columns: Document, Page; and PRE CONTEXT. On the right side of HEADWORD is POST CONTEXT column.

Following the initial concordance of the lexical label of the concept 'colour' in KR *'chromodynamics'*, the learner notices the frequent co-occurrence of 'colour' and 'quark' (Figure 3). Subsequent semantic searches aim at discovering concepts that are co-occurring with *'colour'* (and their relations), and may include the following inquiries:

- Co-occurrence of *'colour'*, *'quark'* and *'gluon'* (Figure 4)
- Further co-occurrences: *'colour'*, 'quark', 'gluon' *'red'*, *'blue'*, *'green'* (Figure 5)

Figure 2. Concordance: Semantic search of Headword 'colour' in KR = 'chromodynamics'

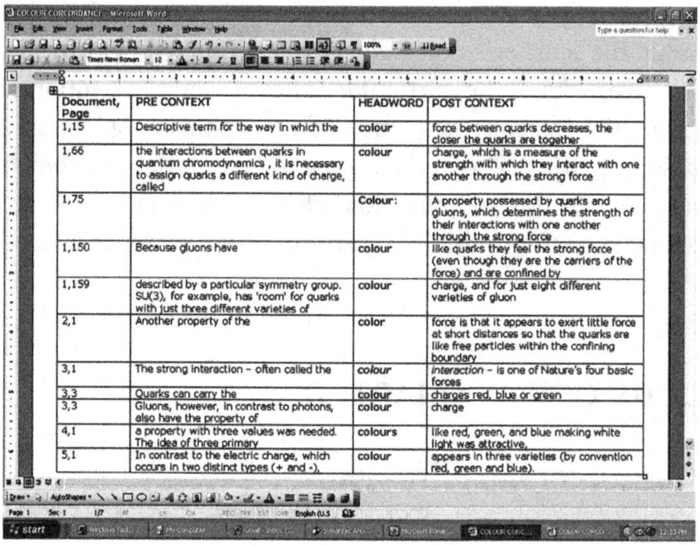

Document, Page	PRE CONTEXT	HEADWORD	POST CONTEXT
1,15	Descriptive term for the way in which the	colour	force between quarks decreases, the closer the quarks are together
1,66	the interactions between quarks in quantum chromodynamics , it is necessary to assign quarks a different kind of charge, called	colour	charge, which is a measure of the strength with which they interact with one another through the strong force
1,75		Colour:	A property possessed by quarks and gluons, which determines the strength of their interactions with one another through the strong force
1,150	Because gluons have	colour	like quarks they feel the strong force (even though they are the carriers of the force) and are confined by
1,159	described by a particular symmetry group. SU(3), for example, has 'room' for quarks with just three different varieties of	colour	charge, and for just eight different varieties of gluon
2,1	Another property of the	color	force is that it appears to exert little force at short distances so that the quarks are like free particles within the confining boundary
3,1	The strong interaction – often called the	*colour*	*interaction* – is one of Nature's four basic forces
3,3	Quarks can carry the	colour	charges red, blue or green
3,3	Gluons, however, in contrast to photons, also have the property of	colour	charge
4,1	a property with three values was needed. The idea of three primary	colours	like red, green, and blue making white light was attractive,
5,1	In contrast to the electric charge, which occurs in two distinct types (+ and -),	colour	appears in three varieties (by convention red, green and blue).

Figure 3. Co-occurrence: follow-up semantic search of Key Word In Context (KWIC) of Headword 'colour' and 'quark' in KR = 'chromodynamics'

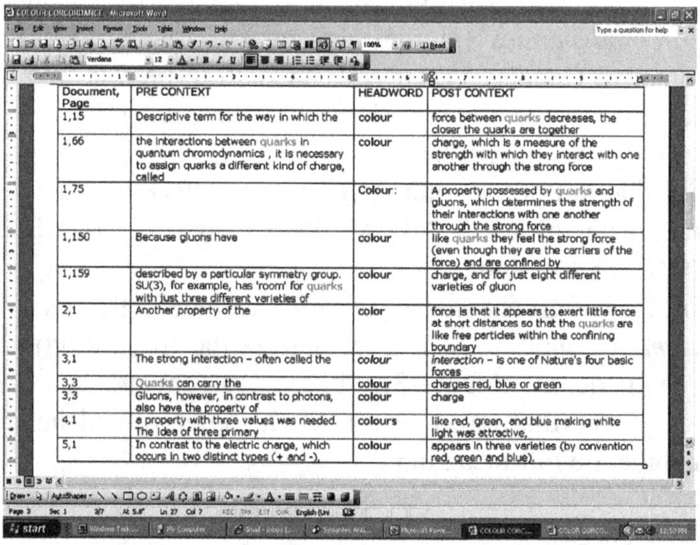

Document, Page	PRE CONTEXT	HEADWORD	POST CONTEXT
1,15	Descriptive term for the way in which the	colour	force between quarks decreases, the closer the quarks are together
1,66	the interactions between quarks in quantum chromodynamics , it is necessary to assign quarks a different kind of charge, called	colour	charge, which is a measure of the strength with which they interact with one another through the strong force
1,75		Colour:	A property possessed by quarks and gluons, which determines the strength of their interactions with one another through the strong force
1,150	Because gluons have	colour	like quarks they feel the strong force (even though they are the carriers of the force) and are confined by
1,159	described by a particular symmetry group. SU(3), for example, has 'room' for quarks with just three different varieties of	colour	charge, and for just eight different varieties of gluon
2,1	Another property of the	color	force is that it appears to exert little force at short distances so that the quarks are like free particles within the confining boundary
3,1	The strong interaction – often called the	*colour*	*interaction* – is one of Nature's four basic forces
3,3	Quarks can carry the	colour	charges red, blue or green
3,3	Gluons, however, in contrast to photons, also have the property of	colour	charge
4,1	a property with three values was needed. The idea of three primary	colours	like red, green, and blue making white light was attractive,
5,1	In contrast to the electric charge, which occurs in two distinct types (+ and -),	colour	appears in three varieties (by convention red, green and blue).

Figure 4. Co-occurrence of Headword 'colour' with 'quark' and 'gluon' in KR = 'chromodynamics'

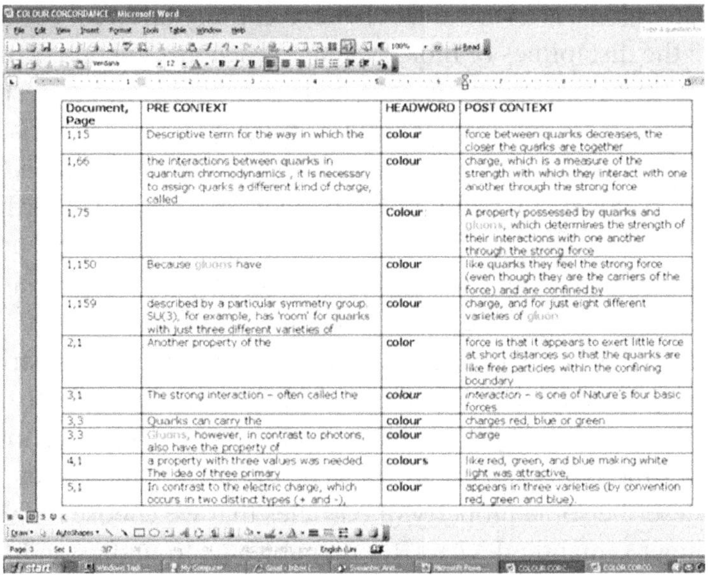

COLOUR CONCORDANCE - Microsoft Word

Document, Page	PRE CONTEXT	HEADWORD	POST CONTEXT
1,15	Descriptive term for the way in which the	**colour**	force between quarks decreases, the closer the quarks are together
1,66	the interactions between quarks in quantum chromodynamics , it is necessary to assign quarks a different kind of charge, called	**colour**	charge, which is a measure of the strength with which they interact with one another through the strong force
1,75		**Colour**	A property possessed by quarks and gluons, which determines the strength of their interactions with one another through the strong force
1,150	Because gluons have	**colour**	like quarks they feel the strong force (even though they are the carriers of the force) and are confined by
1,159	described by a particular symmetry group. SU(3), for example, has 'room' for quarks with just three different varieties of	**colour**	charge, and for just eight different varieties of gluon
2,1	Another property of the	**color**	force is that it appears to exert little force at short distances so that the quarks are like free particles within the confining boundary
3,1	The strong interaction – often called the	***colour***	*interaction* – is one of Nature's four basic forces
3,3	Quarks can carry the	**colour**	charges red, blue or green
3,3	Gluons, however, in contrast to photons, also have the property of	**colour**	charge
4,1	a property with three values was needed. The idea of three primary	**colours**	like red, green, and blue making white light was attractive,
5,1	In contrast to the electric charge, which occurs in two distinct types (+ and -),	**colour**	appears in three varieties (by convention red, green and blue).

Figure 5. Co-occurrence of Headword 'colour' with 'quark', 'gluon' 'red', 'blue', 'green', in KR = 'chromodynamics'

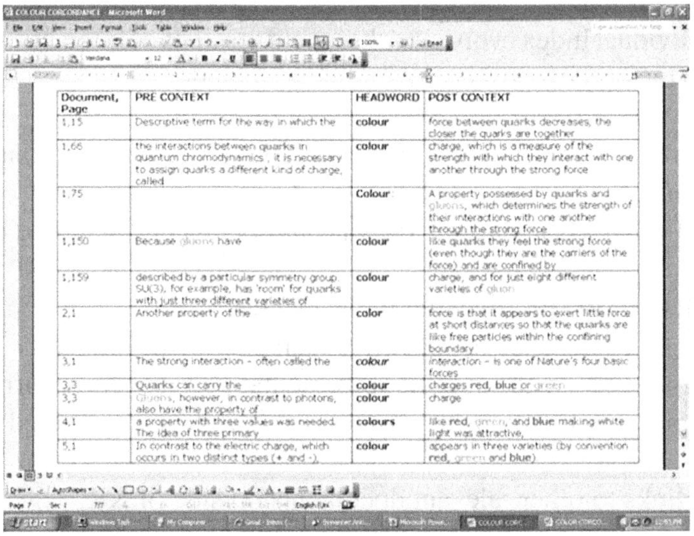

COLOUR CONCORDANCE - Microsoft Word

Document, Page	PRE CONTEXT	HEADWORD	POST CONTEXT
1,15	Descriptive term for the way in which the	**colour**	force between quarks decreases, the closer the quarks are together
1,66	the interactions between quarks in quantum chromodynamics , it is necessary to assign quarks a different kind of charge, called	**colour**	charge, which is a measure of the strength with which they interact with one another through the strong force
1,75		**Colour**	A property possessed by quarks and gluons, which determines the strength of their interactions with one another through the strong force
1,150	Because gluons have	**colour**	like quarks they feel the strong force (even though they are the carriers of the force) and are confined by
1,159	described by a particular symmetry group. SU(3), for example, has 'room' for quarks with just three different varieties of	**colour**	charge, and for just eight different varieties of gluon
2,1	Another property of the	**color**	force is that it appears to exert little force at short distances so that the quarks are like free particles within the confining boundary
3,1	The strong interaction – often called the	***colour***	*interaction* – is one of Nature's four basic forces
3,3	Quarks can carry the	**colour**	charges **red**, **blue** or green
3,3	Gluons, however, in contrast to photons, also have the property of	**colour**	charge
4,1	a property with three values was needed. The idea of three primary	**colours**	like **red**, green, and **blue** making white light was attractive,
5,1	In contrast to the electric charge, which occurs in two distinct types (+ and -),	**colour**	appears in three varieties (by convention **red**, green and **blue**)

SOLUTIONS AND RECOMMENDATIONS

We note that 'colour' is a lexical label of two entirely different superordinate concepts in the disciplines of biology and physics that encode two different meanings in the contexts of *'vision'* and *'chromodynamics'* respectively. Drilling down to a deeper level of building blocks reveals a surprise: in both cases, namely, in the context *vision,* and in the context *chromodynamics,* 'the next level down' of building blocks contains three sub-ordinate co-occurring concepts with the identical lexical labels 'red', 'green' and 'blue'. We all know that these lexical labels were used since antiquity as features of colour vision. How did the same identical lexical labels come to be used in chromodynamics in modern physics? Describing the pioneering work on quantum chromodynamics in the mid-1960s, Gribbin (1999) says: "We stress that the terminology is no more than a convenient semantic device, used to label the quarks—just as, indeed, the use of the words 'up' and 'down' to describe some property of particles that we choose to label 'spin' is a convenient semantic device. But it enables us to understand that there is a difference between a red up quark and a blue up quark, just as there is a difference between a red up quark and a red down quark" (p. 369).

Learner Individual Index

Learner Individual Index evolve in subsequent sessions of Interactive Concept Discovery (InCoD) in a course of study that include:

- Evolving alphabetic list of discovered building blocks (concepts and relations).
- Hyperlinks to paragraphs in the various documents identified by InCoD in KR.
- Annotations to specific paragraphs in a document.
- Ranking of relevance of specific documents to the course.
- Concept map with graphic representations of co-occurrences of concepts and hierarchical and lateral links of discovered building blocks.
- Hyperlinks to other relevant documents outside of KR.

Figure 6 shows a sample of an individual learner's Individual Index for KR = 'Chromodynamics', updated on April 24, 2007.

Figure 6. Learner Individual Index of super-ordinate concept 'colour' in KR = 'chromodynamics'

Latest: April 24, 2007

Content word	Document	Page/Ranking/Annotation
Blue	3	3/R/A
...		
Colour	1	15, 66, 75/R, 150, 159/R/A
...		
Gluon	1	75/R, 150, 159/R
...		
Green	3	3/R/A
...		
Quark	1	15, 66, 75/R, 150, 159/R
	2	1
...		
Red	3	3/R/A

For each found content word (i.e., sub-ordinate concepts and relations), this Learner Individual Index shows: document/page; relevance ranking (scale 1 – 5); annotation.

Individual Learners' Indexes are continuously available to the course instructor. They provide valuable background for private conversations – tete-a-tete and online - between learner and instructor.

Figure 7. Learner evolving concept map of building blocks of super-ordinate concept 'colour' in KR = 'chromodynamics'

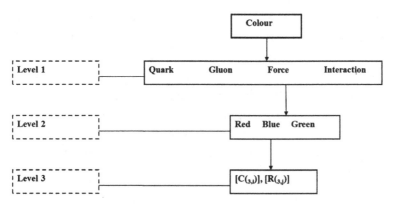

Concepedia (Conceptual Encyclopedia)

Use of information and communication technologies has steadily increased in educational institutions with new pedagogical possibilities and open opportunities for educational interactivity. They have changed the boundaries and limitations of teaching and learning, and have become essential components of modern teaching and learning. E-Learning web-based asynchronous discussion forums are used to complement traditional methods and techniques, and provide virtual environments supporting debate among students, as well as between teacher and student. The asynchronous nature of online discussion forums where all participants are not required to be present or logged on at the same time, allows students flexibility of time and place of their own choice. Small group discussion forums also encourage student-teacher interactions, dialogues, and social interactions to occur outside of a traditional classroom, and allow discussion forums to supplement face-to-face interaction in large undergraduate courses. Asynchronous forums allows students to have more time to structure and organize their thoughts before asking a question or making a statement in class, and students can communicate simultaneously or even participate in multiple discussions at the same time. Some suggest that discussion forums create a more comfortable environment for students to engage in discussion. Because of the reduced social cues within the discussion forum, students feel less threatened to express their views or to ask for help from teachers and peers. Enhanced communication in discussion forums may be especially important because of the type of learning that occur as a function of the discussions and interacting with one another. Namely, what happens is not accumulation of static knowledge, but participating in a creative cognitive process, coming up with ideas, exposing these ideas to others' comments and criticisms, and being able to reshape collaborative knowledge construction: students collaboratively develop and explore in light of peer discussions. Through these social and cognitive processes regarding hypotheses, negotiate differing perspectives, work towards common understandings, and learning outcomes are enhanced by constructing shared meanings. This enhance learning outcomes (Shafrir, Etking & Treviranus, 2006).

Joordans and his associate (Paré & Joordens, 2008; Cheng, Paré, Collimore, & Joordens, 2011) developed peerScholar system to address the need for writing and critical thinking assessments in a specific class setting; the Introductory Psychology course at the University of Toronto Scarborough that has enrolments of over 2000 students per year. Prior to the introduction of peerScholar, assessments were based solely on multiple-choice exams. The challenge was to return the desired writing components to the course and after consideration, the notion of online peer assessment held a high level of promise. "The peerScholar system is an automated online tool used by instructors to manage required readings, writing pieces, assessments, and results for student assignments – all through one Web-based interfac. Each peerScholar assignment can be fully customized by an instructor, but is always broken into three logical phases emphasizing specific tasks. The first phase involves reading and writing tasks that encourage critical thinking and communication skills. The second phase is where the peer assessment process takes place. Finally, the third phase consists of providing students with the assignment results and feedback. Phase durations are specified by the instructor. Each phase, though housed within the same application, is treated as a separate entity with the second phase opening only after the first closes and the third opening after the second closes. Details of each phase are discussed in the following section."

CONCLUSION

Unlike peerScholar, Concepedia evolve through weekly aggregations by the course instructor of Cumulative Index of search activities of all students in the class, who use InCoD semantic searches to access and explore conceptual content in the course KR.

Concepedia is a novel approach to collaborative blended/online learning through shared knowledge of communities of learners that allow individual learners to keep track of their own sequential searches, and to mark, save, and rank documents by their degree of relevance-of-meaning to the conceptual situation under consideration. Concepedia provides a detailed index of content words (lexical labels of concepts and their relations) in KR, including: Frequency and content of annotations on content in locations within specific documents; learners' rankings of documents; learners annotations; as well as learners' commentaries on other learners' annotations. Concepedia encodes the conceptual content of the collective knowledge of a community of learners.

Concepedia is available to all students in the course, and provide valuable background for online and offline conversations among learners, as well as between learners and instructor (Figure 8).

Figure 8. Concepedia of super-ordinate concept 'colour' in KR = 'chromodynamics'

Latest: April 24, 2007

Content word	Document	Page/Ranking	Frequency
Blue	3	3/R	10
...			
Colour	1	15, 66, 75/R, 150, 159/R	35
...			
Gluon	1	75, 150, 159/R	28
...			
Green	3	3/R	10
...			
Quark	1	15, 66, 75, 150, 159/R	28
	2	1	12
...			
Red	3	3/R	10

Interactive Concept Discovery (InCoD) support and facilitate deep comprehension of conceptual content:

- InCoD semantic search of lexical label of a concept in context in the Knowledge Repository of a course provide multiple representations of conceptual situations in different documents composed by different authors, in which the concept under scrutiny is explicitly implicated; this encourages learners to pay attention to equivalence-of-meaning across different representations, and facilitates probing for deeper roots (building blocks) of the concept.
- Unlike searches of structured text documents with pre-defined ontologies embedded in their tags, InCoD identify and codify emerging concepts as well as tacit knowledge that key knowledge holders and subject matter experts may not be explicitly aware of, thus enhancing learning outcomes.
- In contrast to certain currently available portals and databases (e.g., Medline; Web of Knowledge; Scopus; Science Direct) that may restrict searches to metadata – titles, names of authors, and abstracts of included documents - InCoD's use of text analysis tools provide comprehensive results of full text semantic searches.

- Unlike image searches (e.g., photos; plans; scans; diagrams) that are limited to pre-defined metadata keywords embedded in their tags, InCoD directly identify co-occurring concepts and relations appearing in relevant text documents in the KR.

REFERENCES

Cheng, C. K., Paré, D. E., Collimore, L. M., & Steve Joordens, S. (2011). Assessing the effectiveness of a voluntary online discussion forum on improving students course performance. *Computers & Education, 56*(1), 253–261. doi:10.1016/j.compedu.2010.07.024

Gribbin, J. (1999). Q is for quantum: particle physics from A-Z. London: Phoenix Giant.

Paré, D. E., & Joordens, S. (2008). Peering into large lectures: Examining peer and expert mark agreement using peerScholar, an online peer assessment tool. *Journal of Computer Assisted Learning, 24*(6), 526–540. doi:10.1111/j.1365-2729.2008.00290.x

Shafrir, U., Etkind, M., & Treviranus, J. (2006). eLearning Tools for ePortfolios. In Ali Jaffari and Catherine Kauffman (Eds.), *Handbook of Research on ePortfolios* (pp. 206-216). Hershey, PA: Idea Group.

Chapter 7
Meaning Equivalence Reusable Learning Objects (MERLO)

ABSTRACT

In the chapter we discuss Meaning Equivalence Reusable Learning Objects (MERLO), a multi-dimensional database that allow sorting and mapping of important concepts in a given knowledge domain through multi-semiotic representations in multiple sign systems, including: exemplary target statements of particular conceptual situations, and relevant other statements. MERLO pedagogy guides sequential teaching/learning episodes in a course by focusing learners' attention on meaning. The format of MERLO assessment item allow the instructor to assess deep comprehension of conceptual content by eliciting responses that signal learners' ability to recognize, and to produce, multiple representations, in multiple sign-systems - namely, multi-semiotic - that share equivalence-of-meaning. Exposure of scholars and learners to multi-semiotic inductive questions enhance cognitive control of inter-hemispheric attentional processing and enhance higher-order thinking. It highlights the important role of representational competence in scholarship, teaching and learning.

DOI: 10.4018/978-1-5225-2176-1.ch007

INTRODUCTION

Boundary-of-Meaning (BoM) of a Target Statement (TS) is a good measure of the depth of understanding in a given knowledge domain. It documents the results of comparing TS to other representations by two different criteria:

- Surface Similarity (SS) to the Target Statement.
- Meaning Equivalence (ME) with the Target Statement.

MERLO is a multi-dimensional database that allows the sorting and mapping of important concepts in a given knowledge domain through multi-semiotic representations in multiple sign systems, including: exemplary target statements of particular conceptual situations, and relevant other statements.

Figure 1 is a template for constructing an item family of MERLO assessment items anchored in a single target statement TS. Collectively, MERLO item families encode the conceptual mapping that covers the full content of a course - a particular content area within a discipline, for example 'calculus' in mathematics (Figure 2).

Figure 1. Template for constructing an item-family in MERLO

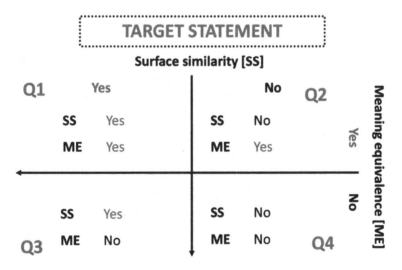

MERLO: Item family

Figure 2. Example of a multi-semiotic MERLO item (mathematics/calculus)

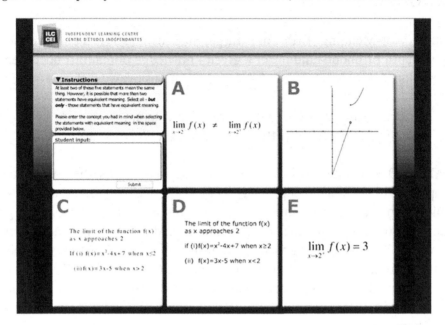

MAIN TOPICS OF THE CHAPTER

Issues, Controversies, Problems

MERLO pedagogy guides sequential teaching/learning episodes in a course by focusing learners' attention on meaning. The format of a MERLO assessment item allows the instructor to assess deep comprehension of conceptual content by eliciting responses that signal learners' ability to recognize, and to produce, multiple representations, in multiple sign-systems - namely, multi-semiotic - that share equivalence-of-meaning.

A typical MERLO assessment item contains 5 unmarked statements: unmarked TS (target statement); plus four additional (unmarked) statements A B C D E from quadrants Q2; Q3; and Q4. Our experience has shown that inclusion of statements from quadrant Q1 makes a MERLO item too easy, because it gives away the shared meaning due to the valence-match between surface similarity and meaning equivalence - a strong indicator of shared meaning between a Q1 and TS. Therefore, Q1 statements are excluded from MERLO assessment items.

Task instructions for MERLO assessment are:

At least two out of these five statements – *but possibly more than two* – share equivalence-of-meaning.

1.   Mark all statements – *but only those* – that share equivalence-of meaning.
2.   Formulate and write down briefly the reasons that guided you in making these decisions.

Figure 2. is an example of MERLO assessment item used at Independent Learning Center (ILC) of TVOntario, a distance education/e-learning high school. The MERLO database for grades 11-12 calculus course was developed by master mathematics teachers who participated in a workshop 'Learning in the Digital Age with Meaning Equivalence Reusable Learning Objects (MERLO) and Interactive Concept Discovery (InCoD)' in 2006-2007, following detailed concept mapping. It is a multi-semiotic MERLO item in the following sign systems: symbolic mathematical equations A and E; visualization/diagram B; language and symbolic mathematical equations C and D.

Figure 3 is an example of a MERLO item in 2nd year course on history of architecture at Ryerson University. It includes 5 representations (at least two of which share equivalence-of-meaning), in the following sign-systems: urban plan A; photograph B; orthogonal drawing C; language D; 3D sketch E.

Learner's response to a MERLO item combines two formats: (i) multiple-choice/multiple-response (recognition) format; and (ii) short answer

Figure 3. Example of a multi-semiotic MERLO item (history of architecture)

(production). Subsequently, there are two scores for each MERLO item: recognition score; and production score.

MERLO Diagnostics of Misconceptions

Each individual student's data profile shows scores of MERLO weekly quizzes, mid-term tests, and final exams in individual courses. These scores identify specific deficits in conceptual understanding of course content, expressed as lower individual Q2 and Q3 scores, and document corrective interventions with individual learners.

Class data profiles show mean MERLO scores in weekly quizzes, as well as mid-term tests, and final exams. This data indicates class specific deficits, expressed as lower mean Q2 and Q3 class scores in conceptual understanding of particular course content, and may prompt the instructor to revisit this content in future lectures or other class activities. These inter-related learning-process data are collected continuously, not just in a particular class, but across all learning and teaching activities throughout the semester and the academic year.

They are continuously available through Concept Science Evidence-Based MERLO Learning Analytics to the learners and to the teachers. Eventually, and subject to strict privacy procedures that protect individual student identity and privacy, these learning analytics are available to the academic institutions.

FUTURE RESEARCH DIRECTIONS

The Concept Science Evidence-Based MERLO Learning Analytics educational informatics system described above evolved since 2002 through sequential stages of development, testing, validation, and implementation of Pedagogy for Conceptual Thinking and Peer Cooperation (Etkind, Kenett, & Shafrir, 2010; Etkind & Shafrir, 2011; 2012; 2014; Shafrir & Etkind, 2006).

Our experience in implementing this novel pedagogy include educational institutions, governmental and private organizations, and health care services.

- Ontario Institute for Studies in Education of University of Toronto (OISE/UT).
- Faculty of Engineering and Architectural Science at Ryerson University.
- George Brown College, Toronto.

- Russian Academy of Sciences – Lycee, Ioffe Physico-Technical Institute, St. Petersburg.
- Independent Learning Center (ILC) of TVOntario.
- Material and Manufacturing Ontario (MMO) Centre of Excellence.
- Roots and Routes Summer Institute - RRSI-2012, at University of Toronto, Scarborough.
- Meir Medical Center, Kfar Saba, Israel.
- Mount Sinai Hospital, Toronto.
- M@t.abel Italian national mathematics educational program, coordinated academically by the Department of Mathematics at University of Turin.

These implementations include workshops for training of instructors and librarians, as well as classroom implementations that cover several knowledge domains, including:

- Language (ESL; learning disabilities).
- Social science (psychology; teacher education).
- History.
- Architecture.
- Mathematics (algebra; geometry; statistics).
- Science (physics; chemistry; biology).
- Medicine (Evidence Based Informed Consent (EBIC) in obstetrics and gynecology).
- Business (project management; risk management)..

Specific comprehension deficits are identified as *depressed recognition scores on quadrants Q2 and Q3* due to the mismatch between the valence of surface similarity and meaning equivalence in these quadrants (Figure 2 of Chapter 5).

In a proof-of-concept implementation of MERLO pedagogy by Material and Manufacturing Ontario (MMO) Center of Excellence (Shafrir & Krasnor, 2002), the explicit goal was to evaluate the potential of MERLO to assess and improve learning outcomes of future courses and workshops in pre-competitive skills to be offered by MMO and the University of Toronto Innovation Foundation. 'Risk management in the supply chain' course was designed and anchored in concept mapping, and delivered by the instructor with guidance and help of the MERLO team. Eighty-one concepts were identified, carefully formulated, and served as the conceptual content of the course. A MERLO database, anchored in these 81 concepts, each formulated as a Target Statement, was constructed for the course. This database guided the delivery of the course content to 20 participants, including self-scoring MERLO quizzes for each of the four classroom sessions of the course. Course design and, in particular, concept mapping and the construction of the database, was done manually, mostly through extensive use of e-mail. Mean scores (proportion correct) for Q2 statements in three consecutive online self-scoring weekly quizzes increased significantly from 0.71 (SD=0.14) to 0.85 (SD=0.12) to 0.95 (SD+0.09) for tests #1, #2, and #3, respectively. The enhancement of learning outcomes in Q2 statements across the three self-scoring tests shows that:

- Recognition of statements with shared equivalence-of-meaning is a learnable skill.
- It is greatly facilitated by detailed feedback, provided through self-scoring and peer cooperation.
- Consistent improvement in Q2 scores means that learners were successful in learning to distinguish between 'surface similarity' and 'meaning equivalence', which allowed them to recognize statements that 'look different' but share meaning with the target statement.

Mean scores for Q3 statements (proportion correct) in this course, with a variation in the range 0.82 to 0.84, showed no significant improvements across tests. It seems that, unlike the situation with Q2 statements discussed above, when encountering Q3 statements, learners were quite skilled at separating 'surface similarity' from 'meaning equivalence.' This allowed learners to recognize and exclude (not choose) Q3 statements already in test #1. However, this skill did not improve with the availability of detailed feedback after self-scoring and peer cooperation as the tests progressed.

SOLUTIONS AND RECOMMENDATIONS

Implementation of pedagogy for conceptual thinking with MERLO formative and summative assessments was presented at European Network for Business and Industrial Statistics (ENBIS-2016) by researchers at the Ministry of Public Education and Department of Mathematic, University of Turin Italy: 'Assessing the level of conceptual understanding of students is both a statistical and a pedagogical challenge. In the context of Mathematics and

Statistics, teachers need to be able to effectively convey concepts to students and feedback on their work is critical information. Experience gained in Italian secondary schools using a novel approach for assessing conceptual understanding called MERLO (Meaning Equivalence Reusable Learning Objects). MERLO is a didactic and methodological tool to emphasize a pedagogical focus on conceptual understanding. What we call 'MERLO pedagogy' is composed of structured activities covering specific concepts within a discipline, through multi-semiotic representations in multiple sign systems as elements of items to be solved by the students, along with specific teaching practices and methodologies to be applied by the teacher with the students. The innovation in MERLO consists of directly challenging students in discovering deep relations among different representations, and not in simply stating if they are true or false, or relate to each other because they are similar in appearance. The teaching innovation is the design of these items by teacher educators, researchers, and teachers, according to MERLO pedagogy. Our research focus on MERLO student scores with results that can be generalized in the general context of statistical education. We compare performance of different classes, the advantage of group exercises and how one can identify the level of conceptual understanding of different concepts. This study shows how to meet the statistical challenge of measuring the level of understanding of students with implications on how Statistics can be taught' (Trichero et al. 2016).

MERLO Statistics in Learning Analytics for Individual Students

MERLO statistics for weekly quizzes for formative assessments, as well as mid-term and final exams summative assessments, are reported for each individual student in every course. They include individual MERLO scores that measure the depth of understanding of each concept in the course content.

Interpretations of depressed Q2 and Q3 scores are very different:

- *A depressed score on Q2* indicates that the learner *fails to include* within the Boundary of Meaning (BoM) of the concept (Shafrir & Etkind, 2005; 2014) certain statements that *do share equivalence-of-meaning* (but do not share surface similarity) with the target. *Such depressed Q2 score signals an over-restrictive (too exclusive) understanding of the meaning of the concept.*

- *A depressed score on Q3* indicates that the learner *fails to exclude* from the Boundary of Meaning (BoM) of the concept certain statements that *do not share equivalence of-meaning* (but that do share surface similarity) with the target. *Such depressed Q3 score signals an under-restrictive (too inclusive) understanding of the meaning of the concept.*

Production score of MERLO test items is based on the clarity and accuracy of the learner's written description of the conceptual situation described in the item, and the explicit inclusion in that description of lexical labels of relevant and important concepts and relations.

Thus, recognition and production scores provide teachers and learners with clear and reliable evidence for depth of understanding, diagnosing misconceptions, and provide clues for remediation.

Cognitive Control of Inter-Hemispheric Attentional Processing of Multi-Semiotic Representations

Communication and relationship between ideas and bodily activities such as processes in the brain were investigated by the philosopher and mathematician Rene Descartes in the 17th century, in what has since been referred to as *mind-body dualism* (Descartes, 1649/1989). Subsequently, the role of the brain in processing information, including acquisition of knowledge, generating ideas, and learning, has been the topic of continuous interest to philosophers and scientists: 'Ideas do not float abstractly in the world. Ideas can be created only by, and only instantiated in, brains. Particular ideas have to be generated by neural structures in brains, and in order for that to happen, exactly the right kind of neural processes must take place in the brain's neural circuitry. Given that image schemas are conceptual in nature – that is, they constitute ideas with a structure of very special kind – they must arise through neural circuitry of a very special kind' (Lakoff & Núñez, 2000; p. 33).

Recent research in neuroscience and brain imaging reveal the benefits of enhancing cognitive/executive control of inter-hemispheric collaboration in the human lateralized brain. 'The terms "cognitive control" or "executive control" summarize a set of cognitive functions that enable an individual to cope with cognitive challenges… for example, to solve complex problems, to plan and monitor goal-directed behavior, to carry out tasks containing multiple parts... the ability to monitor and resolve cognitive conflicts that emerge during these processes is a key aspect of cognitive control' (Westerhausen & Hugdahl, 2010, p. 469; see also: Wickens & McCarley, 2008, p. 146; Vandierendonck et al., 2007).

Published results in neuroscience and brain imaging journals of research on cognitive control include numerous studies, by different researchers, in different experimental contexts. Following is a brief summary of research relevant to Concept Parsing Algorithms (CPA) and to Meaning Equivalence Reusable Learning Objects (MERLO).

Increase in Task Processing Complexity is Facilitated by Engaging Both Hemispheres

The idea that the brain deals with computational complexity by recruiting resources from both hemispheres is receiving confirmation from brain imaging studies... as computational complexity increases, activation that was restricted to a single hemisphere appears to spread across both' (Banich, 2002, p. 290); 'the division of labor between the two hemispheres can increase the overall processing capacity of the brain' (Patel & Hellige, 2007, p. 125; Hellige, 2008).

Inter-Hemispheric Collaboration Facilitate Processing of Multi-Semiotic Tasks

'Of particular interest is emerging evidence from neuroimaging that the corpus callosum employs a differentiated role with callosal areas transmitting different types of information depending on the cortical destination of connecting fibers... to achieve an interhemispheric balance between component brain functions, the corpus callosum appears to exert both functional inhibition and excitation' (Schutle & Muller-Oehring, 2010, p. 184). Miller (1996) discuss studies of lateralization of the contents of memory, and claims: 'the right hemisphere has a wider network of semantic associations than the left, and can represent subtleties of meaning more accurately' (p. 109); in reviewing studies of laterality effects for higher cognitive processes, Miller states: 'laterality effects in perceptual experiments are shown best when there is stimulation of both hemispheres by different stimuli' (p. 219).

Cognitive Control of Inter-Hemispheric Attentional Processing Enables Cooperation Between the Hemispheres in Responding to Multi-Semiotic Tasks

'Interhemispheric interaction is posited to aid attentional processing because it allows for a division of labor across the hemispheres, and allows for parallel processing so that operations performed in one hemisphere can be insulated from those executed in the other... the interaction between the cerebral hemispheres, rather than the specific processes performed by each, can influence certain aspects of attentional functioning because these dynamic interactions modulate the processing capacity of the brain' (Banich, 1998, p. 128; 2002; 2009); 'lateralization of specialized areas can require cooperation between hemispheres to produce a fitting response on a variety of tasks/stimuli... metacontrol is the choice mechanism which determines which hemisphere will become dominant during a given sensorimotor or cognitive task, when each hemisphere has access to the relevant stimuli" (van der Knaap et al., 2011); "the early developing asymmetry in cognitive abilities is balanced by later developing executive functions, or cognitive control' (Hamalainen & Takio (2010, p. 417); 'the results of this study support the view... that interhemispheric interaction is a flexible and dynamic process... Rather than arising from top-down task knowledge or experience on previous trials, the degree to which interhemispheric interaction will benefit performance appears to arise from the processing demands of a single trial. This flexibility may be a mechanism for maximizing the processing power of the brain' (Welcome & Chiarello, 2008); 'the mathematically gifted are better at relaying and integrating information between the cerebral hemispheres... this interhemispheric collaboration is a unique functional characteristic of the mathematically gifted brain' (Singh & O'Boyle, 2004, p. 377); a recent fMRI study with structural equation modeling concluded: 'the increased effective connectivity of these frontoparietal regions provides the mathematically gifted with an advantage in performing complex mathematical reasoning problems, perhaps as a byproduct of their enhanced spatial ability, coupled with a related propensity to code information via imagery based representations... the current results suggest that enhanced brain connectivity is a unique brain characteristic of math giftedness (Prescott et al., 2010, p. 286); 'the increase in laterality during words compared with pictures... stresses the dominant contribution of interhemispheric interactions in the emergence of lateralized semantic activation' (Seghier et al., 2011).

Cognitive Control of Inter-Hemispheric Attentional Processing is Trainable

Recent research suggests that a real-time feedback loop in fMRI studies can be used to improve self-regulation in 'circumscribed regions of the brain' (Rota, 2009, p. 343). Robineau and his colleagues (2014, p.1) were 'training healthy participants to control the interhemispheric balance between their left and right visual cortices. This was accomplished by providing feedback based on the difference in activity between a target visual ROI [Region Of Interest] and the corresponding homologue region in the opposite hemisphere. Eight out of 14 participants learned to control the differential feedback signal over the course of 3 neurofeedback training sessions spread over 3 days, i.e., they produced consistent increases in the visual target ROI relative to the opposite visual cortex. Those who learned to control the differential feedback signal were subsequently also able to exert that control in the absence of neurofeedback. Such learning to voluntarily control the balance between cortical areas of the two hemispheres might offer promising rehabilitation approach'.

Enhancing Attentional Processing With Multi-Semiotic MERLO Items

These experimental results demonstrate that exposure of scholars and learners to multi-semiotic inductive questions enhance cognitive control of inter-hemispheric attentional processing in the lateral brain, and enhance higher-order thinking (Banish, 2002; 2009; de la Vega et al., 2016; Ericson et al. 2007). It highlights the important role of *representational competence* in scholarship, teaching and learning, through enhanced abilities to: (i) recognize and trans-code equivalence-of-meaning in multiple, multi-semiotic, representations within and across sign systems; and (ii) re-represent equivalent meaning by incorporating higher-order relations within and/or across different sign systems (Shafrir, 2012; Shafrir & Etkind, 2005; Etkind & Shafrir, 2014). Such abilities make it possible to focus on meaning through comparative analysis of multi-semiotic representations of conceptual situations. It provides strong support for the rationale underlying Pedagogy for Conceptual Thinking and Peer Cooperation, specifically designed to enhance and refine understanding of multi-semiotic representations that share equivalence-of-meaning.

Following numerous evaluative implementations of MERLO pedagogy for conceptual thinking and peer cooperation (Etkind & Shafrir, 2011, 2013;

Etkind, Kenett, & Shafrir, 2010; Shafrir & Etkind, 2006), and results of neuroscience and brain imaging research, we define:

- *Good conceptual thinkers* as those learners who *score high* on both recognition and production in multi-semiotic MERLO assessments.
- *Poor conceptual thinkers* as those learners who *score low* on both recognition and production in multi-semiotic MERLO assessments.

In order to identify good vs. poor conceptual thinkers, we operationalize the above definition as follows: We convert MERLO raw scores for recognition and for production to Z-scores (standard scores with mean = 0.0 and standard deviation = 1.0). Then we define good and poor conceptual thinkers by performing a double median split of their MERLO recognition and production Z-scores in a core course in their discipline of study (for example, course 'History of Architecture' in the discipline of Architecture). Good conceptual thinkers are those who score high (above the median) on both recognition and production Z-scores. In contrast, poor conceptual thinkers are those learners who score low (at or below the median) on both recognition and production Z-scores.

Figure 4 is a diagrammatic representation of these definitions. As can be seen, good conceptual thinkers occupy the *major diagonal* - upper left

Figure 4. Definition of good and poor conceptual thinkers in a final exam in a core course in their discipline

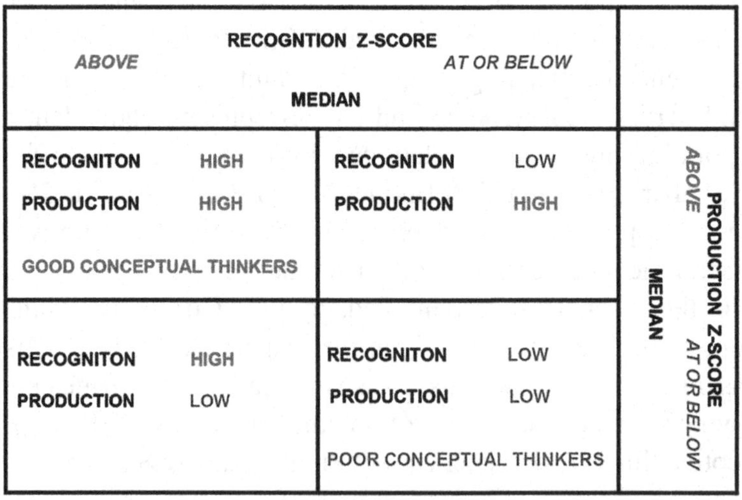

quadrant of the major diagonal of this diagram (*high* in both recognition and in production). Poor conceptual thinkers occupy the lower right quadrant of the major diagonal of this diagram (*low* in both recognition and in production).

The remaining two quadrants are the *minor diagonal,* occupied by 'mixed populations': The upper right quadrant contains learners who are low in recognition and high in production. The lower left quadrant contains learners who are high in recognition and low in production.

An earlier study (Etkind & Shafrir, 2006) investigated the question: Did 'good conceptual thinkers', as defined in Figure 4 above, receive high scores in other courses, and did 'poor conceptual thinkers' receive low scores in other courses? We computed Z-scores for 132 students on MERLO recognition and production scores in final exam in course 'History of Architecture I' 1st year architecture. Double-median split on Z-scores showed that there were 49 'good conceptual thinkers' who scored above the median on both recognition and production; and 44 were 'poor conceptual thinkers' who scored at or below the median on both recognition and production (in addition, there were two mixed groups).

Marks of all students in the other 5 courses, plus mark on an essay in the final exam of the course, were converted to Z-scores. As can be seen in Figure 5, there are consistent differences between good (blue) vs. poor (red) conceptual thinkers in all 5 courses plus History Essay (differences are significant at p $<=0.01$). These results show that MERLO pedagogy for conceptual thinking and peer cooperation identify good and poor conceptual thinkers in a course, as well as across the curriculum.

A recent study tested the hypothesis that enhancing cognitive control of attentional processing of multi-semiotic MERLO items is learnable. Namely, that by participating in weekly multi-semiotic MERLO formative quizzes in large classes, some students who were classified as 'poor conceptual thinkers', developed higher-order thinking skills, and enhance their cognitive control of attentional processing of multi-semiotic MERLO items, become 'good conceptual thinkers'.

Here are specific exemplary results. Out of 140 students registered in architecture course 'ASC 206: Ideas, technology, and precedents I', 30 students were classified in the final exam in May of 2009 as 'poor conceptual thinkers' due to their low (at or below median) Z-scores in a double-media-split on Z-scores MERLO recognition and production (Table 1).

Figure 5. Good vs. Poor conceptual thinkers' z-scores in other courses

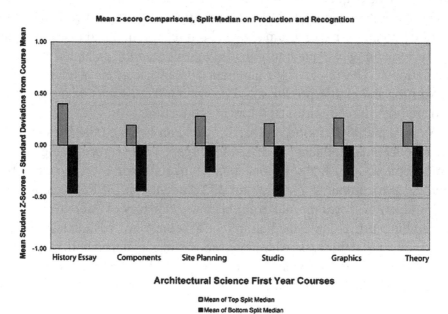

Table 1. Mean z-scores of good vs. Poor conceptual thinkers identified on MERLO items included in final exam of 'ASC 206: Ideas, technology, and precedents I' in May 2009

	MEAN MERLO Z-SCORES 'ASC 206' FINAL EXAM	
	RECOGNITION	**PRODUCTION**
GOOD CONCEPTUAL THINKERS (34 students)	0.81	0.79
POOR CONCEPTUAL THINKERS (30 students)	-0.89	-0.87

Twenty five of those 30 poor conceptual thinkers registered for the second course 'ASC 207: Ideas, technology, and precedents II'. Results of the final exam of this course, in December 2009, revealed that 14 of them improved significantly their Z-scores on recognition and/or production, and *4 of them were elevated from the category of 'poor conceptual thinkers' in May, 2009, to the category of 'good conceptual thinkers' (high on both recognition and production) in December, 2009* (Figure 6).

Figure 6. Of 25 poor conceptual thinkers identified on MERLO items in May 2009, 14 improved their recognition and/or production scores in December 2009; 4 of them became good conceptual thinkers

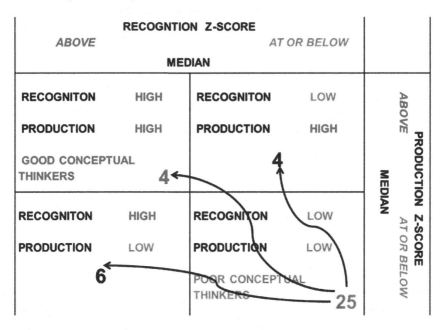

Pedagogy for Conceptual Thinking and Bloom's Taxonomy

Bloom's Taxonomy (Bloom, Krathwohl, & Masia, 1956; Anderson, Krathwohl, & Bloom, 2001) is a broadly accepted categorization of six types of cognitive skills, needed for successfully responding to different types of educational assessments (Figure 7).

Bloom's Taxonomy identifies two groups of cognitive skills: Lower Order Cognitive Skills (LOCS) that include: knowledge, comprehension, and application. And Higher Order Cognitive Skills (HOCS), including: analysis; synthesis; and evaluation. Recent research (Azizian & Ibrahim, 2012; Crowe et al., 2008; Zheng et al., 2008) shows that assessments using multiple-choice and true/false items provide reliable data on students' memorization of facts and procedures (LOCS): 'Is there is a conflict between what undergraduates are being taught and what professional biologists and practicing physicians think students need to master? According to our data, this disjunction may be present in biology courses that assess students using only multiple-choice

Figure 7. Bloom taxonomy: Six levels of thinking skills

BLOOM'S TAXONOMY OF DEVELOPMENT OF THINKING

		LEVEL OF COGNITIVE SKILL	TYPE OF ASSESSMENT
	1	Knowledge	Rote Memory; True/False;
LOCS	2	Comprehension	Multiple-Choice
	3	Application	
	4	Analysis	Interactive Concept Discovery;
HOCS	5	Synthesis	MERLO; Peer cooperation; Essay
	6	Evaluation	

questions and in some traditional medical school curricula' (Zheng et al., p. 415).

Another study of the effects of LOCS vs. HOCS quizzes on learning outcomes in undergraduate biology courses showed that 'students who routinely took quizzes and unit exams requiring higher-order thinking not only showed deeper conceptual understanding by higher scores on high-level questions, but also showed greater retention of the facts, as evidenced by higher scores on low-level questions' (Jensen et al, 2014, p. 317).

Recent studies of conceptual thinking showed that 'Conceptual knowledge is developing a deeper understanding of the mathematical concepts by linking new phenomenon to previously existing phenomenon and understanding the relationships and patterns among these different pieces of information… conceptual knowledge also develops when students connect a newly learned math concept to a previously learned and stored concept' (Agrawal & Morin, 2016, p. 34; see also: Miller & Hudson, 2007).

CONCLUSION

Our evaluative implementations (Etkind, Kennet, & Shafrir, 2016; Shafrir, Etkind, & Treviranus, 2006), showed that the invariant structure of MERLO for encoding knowledge in different disciplines makes it a practical and effective tool for demarcating *Boundary of Meaning (BoM)*, that separate the region which contains representations of a concept that are derivable from multiple CPA definitions from the region containing representations that are not derivable from those definitions. By 'derivable' we mean the construction of multiple representations that are consistent with, and congruent to, CPA formulations, and that, therefore, share equivalence-of-meaning.

Consistent application of CPA lead to representation of conceptual content with clear Boundary of Meaning (BoM) and at a desired level of granularity by:

- Allowing multiple formulations of situations in which a particular super-ordinate concept is explored.
- Guiding the subsequent identification of individual features of alternative sets, each containing features from the three building blocks $\{[C_i], [R_j], [L_k]\}$.
- Facilitating the discovery of deeper roots – features of building blocks of underlying co-occurring sub-ordinate concepts and relations.

Cumulative results of research on Pedagogy for Conceptual Thinking and Peer Cooperation show that Interactive Concept Discovery (InCoD), and Meaning Equivalence Reusable Learning Objects (MERLO) assessment items provide reliable data on students' Higher Order Cognitive Skills (HOCS) of analysis, synthesis and evaluation.

REFERENCES

Agrawal, J., & Morin, L. L. (2016). Evidence-Based Practices: Applications of Concrete Representational Abstract Frameworks across Math Concepts for Students with Mathematics Disabilities. *Learning Disabilities Research & Practice*, *31*(1), 34–44. doi:10.1111/ldrp.12093

Anderson, L. W., Krathwohl, D. R., & Bloom, B. S. (2001). *A Taxonomy for Learning, Teaching, and Assessing: Revision of Bloom's Taxonomy of Educational Objectives*. New York, NY: Longman.

Azizian, U. H., & Ibrahim, F. (2012). Identifying Pupils's Cognitive Level in Fractions Using Bloom's Taxonomy. *International Journal of Business and Social Science*, *3*(9), 254–256.

Banich, M. T. (1998). The missing link: The role of interhemispheric interaction in attentional processing. *Brain and Cognition*, *36*(2), 128–157. doi:10.1006/brcg.1997.0950 PMID:9520311

Banich, M. T. (2002). Interaction between the Hemispheres and its Implications for the Processing Capacity of the Brain. In K. Hugdahl & R. J. Davidson (Eds.), *The Assymetrical Brain* (pp. 261–302). Cambridge, MA: The MIT Press.

Banich, M. T. (2009). Executive Function: The Search for an Integrated Account. *Current Directions in Psychological Research, 18*(2), 89–94. doi:10.1111/j.1467-8721.2009.01615.x

Bloom, B. S., Krathwohl, D. R., & Masia, B. B. (1956). *Taxonomy of Educational Objectives: The Classification of Educational Goals.* New York, NY: D. McKay.

Crowe, A., Dirks, C., & Wenderoth, M. P. (2008). Biology in Bloom: Implementing Blooms Taxonomy to Enhance Student Learning in Biology. *CBE Life Sciences Education, 7*(4), 368–381. doi:10.1187/cbe.08-05-0024 PMID:19047424

de la Vega, A., Chang, L. J., Banich, M. T., Wager, T. D., & Yarkoni, T. (2016). Large-Scale Meta-Analysis of Human Medial Frontal Cortex Reveals Tripartite Functional Organization. *The Journal of Neuroscience, 36*(24), 6553–6562. doi:10.1523/JNEUROSCI.4402-15.2016 PMID:27307242

Descartes, R. (1989). *The Passions of the Souls (translated and annotated by Stephen Voss).* Indianapolis, IN: Hackett Publishing Company. (Original work published 1649)

Ericson, K. I., Colcombe, S. J., Wadhwa, R., Bherer, L., Peterson, M. S., Scalf, P. E., & Kramer, A. F. et al. (2007). Training-Induced Functional Activation Changes in Dual-Task Processing: An fMRI Study. *Cerebral Cortex, 17*(1), 192–204. doi:10.1093/cercor/bhj137 PMID:16467562

Etkind, M., Kenett, R. S., & Shafrir, U. (2010). The evidence-based management of learning: Diagnosis and development of conceptual thinking with meaning equivalence reusable learning objects (MERLO). Invited paper. *Proceedings of the 8th International Conference on Teaching Statistics (ICOTS8).* Ljubljana, Slovenia.

Etkind, M., Kenett, R. S., & Shafrir, U. (2016). Learning in the Digital Age with Meaning Equivalence Reusable Learning Objects (MERLO). In Railean, E., Walker, G., Elçi, A., & Jackson, L. (Eds.), *Handbook of Research on Applied Learning Theory and Design in Modern Education,* pp. 310-333. Hershey PA: IGI Global.

Etkind, M., & Shafrir, U. (2006). Structured eLearning for Depth. IEEE – Computer Society. *Proceedings of the Sixth International Conference on Advanced Learning Technologies (ICALT'06).* doi:10.1109/ICALT.2006.1652592

Etkind, M., & Shafrir, U. (2011). Pedagogy for conceptual thinking: Certificate program for instructors in innovative teaching. *Proceedings of International Conference on Education and New Learning Technologies INTAD 2011*, Barcelona, Spain.

Etkind, M., & Shafrir, U. (2012). Learning Engineering in the Digital Age with Pedagogy for Conceptual Thinking. Proceedings of International Conference on Applied Mathematics and Sustainable Development -Special track SCET-2012, Xi'an, China.

Etkind, M., & Shafrir, U. (2013). Teaching and learning in the digital age with pedagogy for conceptual thinking and peer cooperation. Proceedings of International Association of Technology, Education and Development INTED-2013, Valencia, Spain.

Etkind, M., & Shafrir, U. (2014). Teaching and learning language and content in the digital age with pedagogy for conceptual thinking and Meaning Equivalence Reusable Learning Objects (MERLO). *Proceedings of International Conference ICT for Language Learning*, Florence, Italy.

Hamalainen, H., & Takio, F. (2010). Integrating Auditory and Visual Asymmetry. In K. Hugdahl and R. Westerhausen (Eds.), The Two Halves of the Brain: Information Processing in the Cerebral Hemispheres (pp. 417-438). MIT Press: Cambridge, MASS.

Jensen, J. L., McDaniel, M. A., Woodward, S. M., & Kummer, T. A. (2014). Teaching to the Test… or Testing to Teach: Exams Requiring Higher Order Thinking Skills Encourage Greater Conceptual Understanding. *Educational Psychology Review*, 26(2), 307–329. doi:10.1007/s10648-013-9248-9

Lakoff, G., & Núñez, R. E. (2000). *Where Mathematics Comes From: How the Embodied Mind Brings Mathematics into Being*. Basic Books.

Miller, R. (1996). *Axonal Conduction Time and Human Cerebral Laterality: A Psychobiological Theory*. Amsterdam: Harwood Academic Publishers.

Miller, S. P., & Hudson, P. J. (2007). Using evidence-based practices to build mathematics competence related to conceptual, procedural, and declarative knowledge. *Learning Disabilities Research & Practice*, *22*(1), 47–57. doi:10.1111/j.1540-5826.2007.00230.x

Patel, U. J., & Hellige, J. B. (2007). Benefits of interhemispheric collaboration can be eliminated by mixing stimulus formats that involve different cortical access routes. *Brain and Cognition*, *63*(2), 114–127. doi:10.1016/j.bandc.2006.10.007 PMID:17174457

Prescott, J., Gavrilescu, M., Cunnington, R., OBoyle, M. W., & Egan, G. F. (2010). Enhanced brain connectivity in math-gifted adolescents: An fMRI study using mental rotation. *Cognitive Neuroscience*, *1*(4), 277–288. doi:10.1080/17588928.2010.506951 PMID:24168381

Robineau, F., Rieger, S. W., Mermoud, C., Pichon, S., Koush, Y., van de Ville, D., & Scharnowski, F. et al. (2014). Self-regulation of inter-hemispheric visual cortex balance through real-time fMRI neurofeedback training. *NeuroImage*, *100*, 1–14. doi:10.1016/j.neuroimage.2014.05.072 PMID:24904993

Rota, G. (2009). Direct brain feedback and language learning from the gifted. In G. Dogil & S. M. Reiterer (Eds.), *Language Talent and Brain Activity* (pp. 337–350). Berlin: Mouton de Gruyter.

Schutle, T., & Muller-Oehring, E. M. (2010). Contribution of callosal connections to the interhemispheric integration of visuomotor and cognitive processes. *Neuropsychology Review*, *20*(2), 174–190. doi:10.1007/s11065-010-9130-1 PMID:20411431

Seghier, M. L., Josse, G., Leff, A. P., & Price, C. J. (2011). Lateralization is Predicted by Reduced Coupling from the Left to Right Prefrontal Cortex. *Cerebral Cortex*, *21*(7), 1519–1531. doi:10.1093/cercor/bhq203 PMID:21109578

Shafrir, U. (2012). Representational competence. In I. E. Sigel (Ed.), *The Development of Mental Representation: Theory and Applications.* (pp. 371-389). Mahwah, NJ: Lawrence Erlbaum Publishers.

Shafrir, U., & Etkind, M. (2005). *Concept Parsing Algorithms: Mapping the Conceptual Content of Disciplines. Version 11.0 (January, 2005)*. Toronto: PARCEP.

Shafrir, U., & Etkind, M. (2006). eLearning for depth in the semantic web. *British Journal of Educational Technology, 37*(3), 425–444. doi:10.1111/j.1467-8535.2006.00614.x

Shafrir, U., Etkind, M., & Treviranus, J. (2006). eLearning Tools for ePortfolios. In Ali Jaffari and Catherine Kauffman (Eds.), *Handbook of Research on ePortfolios*, pp. 206-216. Idea Group.

Shafrir, U., & Krasnor, C. (2002). *Risk management in the supply chain: Increasing competitiveness of Ontario's material and manufacturing companies through enhanced training outcomes in pre-competitive skills. Final Report. Ontario Material and Manufactoring (MMO).* Center of Excellence.

Singh, H., & OBoyle, M. W. (2004). Interhemispheric Interaction During Global–Local Processing in Mathematically Gifted Adolescents, Average-Ability Youth, and College Students. *Neuropsychology, 18*(2), 371–377. doi:10.1037/0894-4105.18.2.371 PMID:15099159

Trinchero, G., Arzarello, F., Kenett, R. S., Robutti, O., Carante, P., Shafrir, U., & Etkind, M. (2016). Assessing and Enhancing Conceptual Understanding: A Statistical and Educational Challenge. European Network for Business and Industrial Statistics, Conference Proceedings.

van der Knaap, L. J., Ineke, J. M., & van der Ham, B. (2011). How does the corpus callosum mediate interhemispheric transfer? A review. *Behavioural Brain Research, 223*(1), 211–221. doi:10.1016/j.bbr.2011.04.018 PMID:21530590

Vandierendock, A., & Szmalec, A. Deschuyteneer,& Depoorter, A. (2007). Towards a MulticomponentView of Executive Control. In N. Osaka, R.H. Logie, & M. D'Esposito (Eds.), The Cognitive Neuroscience of Working Memory (pp. 247-249). Oxford University Press.

Welcome, S., & Chiarello, C. (2008). How dynamic is interhemispheric interaction? Effects of task switching on the across-hemisphere advantage. *Brain and Cognition, 67*(1), 69–75. doi:10.1016/j.bandc.2007.11.005 PMID:18206285

Westerhausen, R., & Hugdahl, K. (2010). Cognitive Control of Auditory Laterality. In K. Hugdahl & R. Westerhausen (Eds.), *The Two Halves of the Brain* (pp. 469–497). Cambridge, MA: MIT Press. doi:10.7551/mitpress/9780262014137.003.0350

Wickens, C. D., & McCarley, J. S. (2008). *Applied Attention Theory*. Boca Raton, FL: CRC Press.

Zheng, A. Y., Lawhorn, J. K., Lumley, T., & Freeman, S. (2008). Application of Blooms Taxonomy Debunks MCAT Myth. *Science, 319*(5862), 414–415. doi:10.1126/science.1147852 PMID:18218880

Chapter 8

Concept Science:
Content and Structure of Labeled Patterns in Human Experience

ABSTRACT

This chapter describe the evolution of Concept Science that gave rise to Concept Parsing Algorithms (CPA). Concept Science developed ways to clarify conceptual content encoded in unstructured text that communicate context-specific knowledge in a sublanguage within a discipline. It was developed and tested since the early 1990s at the University of Toronto and Ryerson University in Toronto (Shafrir and Etkind, 2010). Concept Science lead to Pedagogy for Conceptual Thinking with Meaning Equivalence Reusable Learning Objects (MERLO) that offer a powerful tool for engaging and motivating students, and enhancing learning outcomes. This chapter describe some of Concept Science-based tools that provide new ways to discover, encode, and manage knowledge in large digital libraries of unstructured text in educational, governmental, NGO, and business organizations.

INTRODUCTION

Concept Science is an emergent discipline. Its content is the conceptual structure of content of different disciplines, and the different ways in which labeled patterns in human experience are encoded and communicated in different domains of knowledge. The challenge of Concept Science is not

DOI: 10.4018/978-1-5225-2176-1.ch008

the construction of generic semantic tools for discovering literal meanings encoded in natural language. Rather, Concept Science strives to find ways to clarify conceptual content encoded in unstructured text that *communicate context-specific knowledge in a sublanguage within a discipline:* 'Taking conceptual analyses seriously entails demonstrating in any research project as strong a concern for epistemological and ontological issues as for issues of study design, sample characteristics, measurement issues, data collection, and statistical analyses. Deep conceptual issues need to be understood as integral to, and constitutive of, the entire research process, not as peripheral addenda or convenient heuristics' (Overton, 2015).

MAIN FOCUS OF THE CHAPTER

Issues, Controversies, Problems

Concept Science disambiguate meaning encoded in text, by recognizing the distinction between literal meaning of words in general language and the use of words as Lexical Labels of concepts: 'the meaning of a word is its use in the language' (Wittgenstein, 1967, §43); it explicates the role of 'secret codes' that are controlled vocabularies embedded in sublanguages that associate particular Lexical Labels of concepts with well defined meanings within specific contexts in a discipline. Systematic exploration of a controlled vocabulary in context in a discipline, guided by Concept Science principles, reveal the hierarchical and lateral links in the conceptual structure of the discipline, sometimes referred to as the *philosophy of the discipline*: 'In philosophy, the concepts with which we approach the world themselves become the topic of enquiry. A philosophy of a discipline such as history, physics, or law seeks not so much to solve historical, physical, or legal questions, as to study the concepts that structure such thinking, and to lay bare their foundations and presuppositions. In this sense philosophy is what happens when a practice becomes self-conscious.' (Oxford Dictionary of Philosophy, 2005).

On this view, Concept Science, whose goal is to examine knowledge by discovering and mapping the conceptual content and conceptual structure of individual disciplines, as well as to conduct comparative analyses of the conceptual structure of different disciplines, has goals that are similar to those of '*experimental philosophy*' (Alexander & Weinberg, 2007; Kornblith, 2006).

Kornblith believes that in contrast to the traditional view that epistemology and philosophy look to common-sense intuition for guidance when considering the concept of knowledge, the main goal of epistemology and philosophy is actually to examine the conceptual content and structure of disciplines: 'There is no need to examine our pre-theoretical conceptions of what the world is like before we investigate the world itself. The picture of philosophy as a precursor to science, which serves to fix its subject matter puts philosophy to work on a job which does not need doing. If philosophy is to fulfill its ambitions then, and maintain its integrity, we need to stop examining out intuitions and look at the phenomena themselves' (p. 18).

We note that controlled vocabularies in sublanguages exist not only in formal disciplines, in the natural sciences, technology, social sciences, humanities, and professions (e.g., law; accounting; architecture; etc.). Controlled vocabularies in sublanguages exist also in knowledge domains that evolve in organizations where specialization drives discovery of patterns in the data; identify/create lexical labels of concepts that encode well-defined meanings in the context of the organization's content area; and use them to advance the organization's goals.

Concept Science-based tools provide new ways to discover, encode, and manage knowledge in large digital libraries of unstructured text in educational, governmental, NGO, and business organizations.

Concept Science is a systematic and logical approach to the exploration of meanings of concepts (Miller, 1991) that derive from their etymology (Sager, 2000, p. 11) and from particular features contained in their building blocks. Semantic searches guided by Concept Science principles extract meaning from digital text by using text analysis tools that enable and guide the construction of clear definitions of meaning-bearing concepts within particular contexts with clear and explicit criteria, such as embedded in Meaning Equivalence Reusable Learning Objects (MERLO). This allow demarcating Boundary of Meaning (BoM) of Target Statements and judging the degree of commonality-of-meaning of multiple representations of conceptual content. It also enable clear definitions of Conceptual Footprint (CF) of individual documents, and for flexibility in determination of the desired level of Granularity of Meaning (GoM) of textual descriptions of specific conceptual content. As well as for drilling for depth/roots of building blocks of a concept under scrutiny and facilitates identification of hierarchical and lateral links in, and comparative analysis of, conceptual structure in different domains of knowledge.

Shalit (2006) studied deep comprehension of English spatial prepositions in college students; she conducted detailed concept mapping of English spatial prepositions in four categories: Anthropomorphic (e.g. front, back); Inclusion (e.g., in, out); Proximity (e.g., near, close to); and Verticality (e.g., up, down). Native English speakers generally view spatial prepositions as a necessary, non-problematic, over-learned vocabulary in daily use. However, even native English speakers are often confused when presented with nuances of meaning differences between spatial prepositions such as 'beneath' and 'underneath'; for learners with reading disability, or learners whose mother tongue is not English, some 'nuanced' spatial prepositions may present a challenge.

Shalit constructed four MERLO tests (see Figure 1 of Chapter 7), each containing eight item-families in each of the four categories; these MERLO were then used to compose two tests, with 16 items each; both tests were administered to three groups of college students: E1 (English speakers; N=98); ESL (English as a Second Language; N=54); RD (reading disabled; N=55).

The (unmarked) Target Statement in the MERLO item in Table 1 is (C); statement (B) originates in quadrant Q2; statements (A) and (E) originate in quadrant Q3; and statement (D) originates in quadrant Q4.

Shalit's results (Table 2, collapsed over all 32 items) reveal

- Depressed Q2 and Q3 scores in all three groups; within each group, mean proportional scores for Q2 and Q3 statements were significantly lower ($p <= 0.5$) than proportional scores of TS and Q4 statements
- Native English speakers significantly outperformed both the ESL and the RD groups on Q2- and Q3-type statements ($p <= 0.5$), but not on TS and Q4 statements.

Table 1. Example of MERLO assessment item of spatial prepositions of the spatial concept 'near' (Shalit, 2006)

A	That colorful painting hanging north of the fireplace was a gift from Maria and Ian from their trip to Venice.
B	The vibrantly colored painting which is hanging close to the fireplace was a present from Venice given by Ian and Maria
C	That colorful painting hanging near the fireplace was a gift from Ian and Maria from their trip to Venice.
D	The colorful painting comes from Ian and Maria from when they lived in Venice, so it was placed over the fireplace for all to see!
E	That colorful painting hanging nearest the fireplace was a gift to Ian and Maria from their trip to Venice.

Table 2. Mean proportional scores on MERLO 'English spatial prepositions' in college students: Native English speakers (E1); ESL; and reading disabled (RD)

	TS	Q2	Q3	Q4
E1	.85	.76	.79	.93
ESL	.79	.64	.74	.88
RD	.83	.67	.66	.85

SOLUTIONS AND RECOMMENDATIONS

Latent Semantic Analysis (LSA) is a procedure for indexing meaning-similarity of words, sentences and discourse, sometime referred to as Latent Semantic Indexing (LSI) (Deerwester et al., 1990; Landauer, Foltz, & Laham, 1998; see a recent review by Kontostathis & Pottenberg, 2006).

'Latent Semantic Analysis (LSA) is a mathematical/statistical technique for extracting and representing the similarity of meaning of words and passages by analysis of large bodies of text. It uses singular value decomposition, a general form of factor analysis, to condense a very large matrix of word-by-context data into a much smaller, but still large - typically 100-500 dimensional - representation... The similarity between resulting vectors for words and contexts, as measured by the cosine of their contained angle, has been shown to closely mimic human judgments of meaning similarity and human performance based on such similarity in a variety of ways. For example, after training on about 2,000 pages of English text it scored as well as average test-takers on the synonym portion of TOEFL - the ETS Test of English as a Foreign Language... After training on an introductory psychology textbook it achieved a passing score on a multiple-choice exam' (http://lsa. colorado.edu).

Recent research (Evangelopoulos, 2013) provide support for LSA as a reliable tool for modeling meaning: 'In the last two decades, LSA has demonstrated its ability to model various psycho-linguistic phenomena and proven its value as a useful statistical technique for the extraction of meaning from text. LSA has been used by psychologists, cognitive scientists, as well as researchers in education, linguistics, and many other related areas to model cognitive functions such as word meaning, memory, and speech coherence. In this review we summarize some technical details from the LSA literature that include the creation of a latent semantic space, the calculation of similarity metrics among terms and documents, and the interpretation of the latent semantic dimensions. Corresponding computations are illustrated with the help of a small example. Selected software packages that implement these computations are briefly listed as a note at the end of the article. We conclude with the observation that publication activity related to LSA continues at an ever increasing pace, resulting in an increasing interdisciplinary coverage of LSA's application domain, and an increasing level of sophistication and methodological rigor at which it is used in research studies. The goal of this focused introduction is to encourage the reader to explore LSA's strong potential and contribute to its increasing body of knowledge. Limitations of Latent Semantic Analysis include its disregard for sentence-level individual document meaning that stems from word order, which is an inherent limitation of all bag-of-words models, and the scarcity of software solutions that implement LSA. Possible future uses of LSA include tensor (high-order) SVD applications that go beyond term-by-document representations and make use of multi-dimensional spaces and, perhaps, cognitive science applications that focus on the interpretability of the latent semantic space.' (p. 690).

We conducted a study that compare the reliability and validity of Concept Parsing Algorithms (CPA) with Latent Semantic Indexing (LSI) in identifying uniqueness of lexical labels of concepts in context, and in demarcating Boundary of Meaning (BoM). We chose LSI because it is generally accepted as a reliable and valid method for encoding the meaning of concepts in unstructured text and is often used in studies of meaning extraction from corpus-based digital documents (Dominich, 2003; Guo et al., 2003; Wiemer-Hastings, 1999).

Prior to calculating meaning-similarity indices, LSI trains on a well defined large corpus of digital text (i.e., in the above quoted examples, LSI trained on: general English text; and psychology-specific text). We tested LSI in two different ways: First, we tested the hypothesis that LSI supports the core construct of controlled vocabulary in a sublanguage, namely, that Lexical Labels act like proper names of concepts that are recognized patterns in the data. Secondly, we tested the hypothesis that LSI is able to clearly demarcate the Boundary of Meaning (BoM) of Target Statements (TS) that encode particular conceptual situations.

- **LSI Test #1:** Do Lexical Labels act as proper names of concepts?

We used LSI to evaluate the claim regarding the uniqueness of a lexical label of a concept in a sublanguage – a context-within-discipline-specific text;

in other words, the claim that such a lexical label acts like a proper name and does not accept synonyms. This claim generates the following expectations:

- When a lexical label of a concept in a sublanguage is replaced by a synonym it loses its unique meaning in the sublanguage.
- However, when a lexical label is replaced by a synonym - but interpreted within the language at large - it essentially retains its literal meaning.

In order to test these claims we used the psychological concept with the lexical label 'reinforcement'; it is defined in the introductory psychology textbook that was part of the training corpus of LSA in the discipline 'psychology' (Gleitman, Fridlund & Reisberg, 1999): 'Reinforcement refers to strengthening a response by following it with some attractive stimulus or situation' (p. 132).

We asked LSI meaning-similarity indexing engine (accessible through the website: http://lsa.colorado.edu) to compare the meaning of the Lexical Label 'reinforcement' with three different synonyms in 2 different semantic spaces namely, when interpreted (1) within English at 1st year college level; and (2) within a psychology semantic space, based on a corpus that contains the text of three psychology introductory textbooks .

Results (Table 3) show three clear patterns:

- When interprcted in the general context of English versus the sublanguage of the discipline-specific context of psychology, the same synonyms have different meaning-similarity indices (LSI) with the Lexical Label 'reinforcement'.
- All three synonyms to 'reinforcement' retain the meaning in the context of English text much better than in the sublanguage of psychology.

Table 3. LSI comparison of index of meaning-similarity (cosines of contained angle; max = 1.0; min = -1.0) of the lexical label "Reinforcement" with three synonyms in two semantic spaces: 'English' and 'Psychology'

Synonym	English	Psychology
Reinforcing	0.79	0.46
To reinforce	0.46	0.14
To fortify	0.17	-0.03

- LSI of the two synonyms that are derivatives of the same linguistic root as the lexical label 'reinforcement' (i.e., 'reinforcing'; 'to reinforce') are better aligned with 'reinforcement' than a synonym derived from a different linguistic root (i.e., 'to fortify'), both in general English and in psychology; however, in psychology even those synonyms that share a common linguistic root with the lexical label 'reinforcement' show large discrepancies in meaning-similarity.

In summary, LSI lends support to the fundamental claim underlying CPA, namely, that substitution of a synonym for a Lexical Label of a concept in a sublanguage would result in loss of meaning.

- **LSI Test #2:** Can LSI clearly demarcate the Boundary of Meaning (BoM) of Target Statements (TS) that encode particular conceptual situations?

In the second test, we used Shalit's two MERLO tests of deep comprehension of English spatial prepositions described above. In these tests, quadrant specific scores of TS and Q2 signal judgments of meaning similarity, and quadrant specific scores of Q3 and Q4 signal judgments of meaning dissimilarity. A close examination of Table 3 above reveals that:

- Mean quadrant scores of students in the E1, ESL and RD groups that *correctly included* Target Statements in their choices of meaning equivalent statements were 0.85; 0.79; and 0.83; respectively.
- Mean scores for *correctly including* Q2 were 0.76; 0.64; and 0.67 for these groups.
- Mean quadrant scores of E1, ESL and RD students that *correctly excluded* Q3 from their choices of meaning equivalence statements were 0.79; 0.74; and 0.66; respectively.
- Finally, mean scores for *correctly excluding* Q4 from their choices of meaning equivalence statements were 0.93; 0.88; and 0.85 for these groups.

We asked the Latent Semantic Analysis website (http://lsa.colorado. edu) to calculate, for each of the 32 MERLO items in Shalit's two MERLO tests, the meaning-similarity index LSI of the Target Statement compared to each of the four other, thematically-relevant statements in the item. Since these 'four other' statements originated in quadrants Q2; Q3; and Q4, our expectations were that LSI will be high (close to 1.0) for Q2, but low (close to 0.0, or negative) for both Q3 and Q4.

Table 4 shows the mean LSI indexes of similarity-of-meaning (cosine of contained angle) between Target Statements and statements that originated in quadrants Q2, Q3, and Q4, for all 32 items in Shalit's two MERLO tests of deep comprehension of English spatial prepositions.

Although these results are not expressed in the same units as Shalit's proportional quadrant-specific scores (Table 2), it is possible to do a qualitative comparative analysis between these LSI numerical values and Shalit's scores. Such analysis shows the following pattern of results:

- In Q2-type statements, LSI scored 0.80 (Document-to-document) and 0.94 (Term-to-term); this signals a high index of meaning-similarity with TS, and corresponds to Shalit's findings.
- LSI meaning-similarity index for Q3 with TS of 0.94 (Document-to-document) and 0.98 (Term-to-term) is very high, and means that LSI judged Q3 statements not only to be located within the Boundary of Meaning (BoM) of TS, but to be more similar in meaning to TS than Q2 statements.
- Finally, LSI=0.65 (Document-to-document) and 0.93 (Term-to-term) for Q4 statements means that LSI did not exclude these irrelevant statements from BoM.

LSI meaning-similarity indices in Table 4 show that:

1. LSI failed to demarcate the Boundary of Meaning (BoM) of the Target Statements (TS).

Table 4. Mean Latent Semantic Index (LSI) of meaning-similarity (max=1.0) between Target Statement and statements from quadrants Q2, Q3 and Q4 (within-item) in Shalit's 32 MERLO items assessing deep comprehension of English spatial prepositions

QUADRANT OF ORIGIN	LSI Document-to-Document	LSI Term-to-Term
Q2	0.80	0.94
Q3	0.94	0.98
Q4	0.65	0.93

2. LSI consistently produced 'false positives', namely, Q3 statements that LSI incorrectly placed within the Boundary of Meaning of the Target Statements (TS).
3. Similarly, LSI consistently produced 'false negatives', and incorrectly placed Q4 statements within the Boundary of Meaning of the Target Statements (TS).

The results of the two tests reported above are mixed; on the one hand, results of LSI Test #1 were supportive of the fundamental construct underlying CPA, namely, of the uniqueness of meaning attached to Lexical Labels of concepts within a particular sublanguage (context in a discipline). However, results of LSI Test #2 show that LSI consistently failed to demarcate the Boundary of Meaning (BoM) of Target Statements that describe specific content in which English spatial prepositions are involved.

Specifically, LSI included within BoM statements from quadrant Q3 that bear surface similarity to TS (same-similar words, in the same-similar order), but that are not equivalent in meaning to TS. Statements originating in the Q4 quadrant were also wrongfully included by LSI within BoM.

CONCLUSION

In comparison to Concept Parsing Algorithms (CPA), LSI is systematically deficient in indexing meaning similarity between statements that share surface similarity but that do not share equivalence-of-meaning, namely, LSI is deficient in demarcating Boundary of Meaning (BoM) of Target Statements. This is a serious flaw in a methodology that claims to closely mimic human judgments of meaning similarity at the term, sentence, and document levels. These findings highlight the need for further studies of LSI, as well as systematic studies of other meaning modeling algorithms; these studies should document the ability of such algorithms to clearly demarcate Boundary of Meaning (BoM).

Certificate in Concept Parsing Algorithms (CPA) for Instructors and Librarians

A certificate program, developed since 2009 and offered by iSchool Institute - Faculty of Information at University of Toronto, was designed for instructors and librarians in K-12 and post-secondary institutions, as well as in public and private organizations with professional learning programs. This certificate provides hands-on, experiential learning of practical tools for implementation of Conceptual Curation and Concept Parsing Algorithms (CPA) in the classroom. The certificate was developed and implemented at Ontario Institute for Studies in Education of University of Toronto; Faculty of Engineering and Architectural Science at Ryerson University; Russian Academy of Sciences - Ioffe Physico-Technical Institute, St. Petersburg; Material and Manufacturing Ontario (MMO) Centre of Excellence; and Roots and Routes Summer Institute - RRSI-2012, at University of Toronto Scarborough.

The certificate program covers a total of 72 instruction hours, delivered by Uri Shafrir and Masha Etkind, including: instruction; group work; group and individual presentations; and final project presentations. The certificate program covers the following topics:

- **Introduction to Concept Science:** Concepts and conceptual relations: sub-languages with controlled vocabularies; lexical label and building blocks of a concept; Concept Parsing Algorithms (CPA); typology of concepts; multiple definitions of a concept; multi-semiotic representations of a concept across sign systems; evolving concepts; examples from different knowledge domains.
- **Knowledge Repositories (KR):** Networked information of digital full-text documents: type; availability; accessibility http://www.cni. org/ ; construction and use of a Knowledge Repository for a course of study with Zotero; creation of knowledge repositories by scholars and instructors in different knowledge domains; examples from http:// www.oxfordbibliographies.com/ .
- **Semantic Searches:** Key Word In Context (KWIC): concordance; proximity/co-location/co-occurrence; word frequencies; use of KWIC text analysis with Zotero and Voyant tools; Google 'around' operator for proximity search http://googlesystem.blogspot.ca/2010/12/googles-around-operator.html; digital research tools in Bamboo http://dirt. projectbamboo.org/; creation of course KWIC examples by instructors in different knowledge domains.
- **Interactive Concept Discovery (InCoD):** Engaging and motivating students with interactive learning; Learner's Individual Index: annotation; tagging; linking; concept maps; drilling to discover deeper

levels of building blocks of a concept; individual student's learning-curve; Granularity of Meaning (GoM) of a document.

- **Representational Competence:** Review of the literature on semiotics and the development of mental representations; use of different sign systems in various knowledge domains - examples by instructors.

- **Meaning Equivalence Reusable Learning Objects (MERLO):** Structured and unstructured problems as tools for scholarship teaching and learning; multiple representations that share equivalence-of-meaning; template for MERLO item construction: Target Statement (TS), plus (2X2) matrix of Surface Similarity (SS) by Meaning Equivalence (ME); MERLO item types; overview of existing MERLO databases in different knowledge domains, including: physics; mathematics; biology; architecture; psychology; education; project management; business; construction of MERLO databases by instructors for courses in their own knowledge domains.

- **MERLO Formative Classroom Quizzes:** Structure of weekly multi-semiotic MERLO quizzes in the classroom; exploring Boundary of Meaning (BoM) of different representations of conceptual situations; peer cooperation and knowledge of being observed in small group discussions; feedback in class discussions to individual recognition and production responses; construction and administration of in-class MERLO formative assessment by instructors for their courses in different knowledge domains.

- **MERLO in Summative Assessments:** Informational/procedural vs. conceptual comprehension of course content; different formats of 'informational/procedural items' in summative assessment – multiple-choice and true/false; different formats of 'conceptual items' and 'ConcepTests' in summative assessment; scoring of summative assessments by instructors in different knowledge domains; comparative analysis of informational/procedural vs. conceptual knowledge of course content; Bloom Taxonomy.

- **Cognitive Control of Attentional Processing:** Review of recent research in neuroscience and brain imagery on cognitive control of inter-hemispheric attentional processing of multi-semiotic stimuli.

- **CONCEPEDIA (Conceptual Encyclopedia):** Aggregation of Individual Indexes of all students in the course; enhancing individual students reputations as cooperators who contribute to the public good; individual students commentaries on annotations by other students; cumulative process-learning-curve of the class.

- **CF (Conceptual Footprint) of a Document:** Aggregation of all annotations - in Individual Indexes of all students - that are relevant to a particular document in the KR; enhancing individuals' reputations as cooperators who contribute to the public good.
- **Documenting Mastery-of-Knowledge of Individual Learners in e-Portfolios:** MERLO formative classroom quizzes; MERLO summative assessments; Interactive Concept Discovery (InCoD), annotations and tagging; CONCEPEDIA and individual commentaries on annotations by other students.

REFERENCES

Alexander, J., & Weinberg, J. M. (2007). Analytic Epistemology and Experimental Philosophy. *Philosophy Compass*, *2*(1), 56–80. doi:10.1111/j.1747-9991.2006.00048.x

Deerwester, S., Dumais, S. T., Furnas, G. W., Landauer, T. K., & Harshman, R. (1990). Indexing by Latent Semantic Analysis. *Journal of the American Society for Information Science*, 41–46, 391–407.

Dominich, S. (2003). Connectionist Interaction Information Retrieval. *Information Processing & Management*, *39*(2), 167–194. doi:10.1016/S0306-4573(02)00046-8

Evangelopoulos, N. E. (2013). Latent semantic analysis. *Wiley Interdisciplinary Reviews: Cognitive Science*, *4*, 683–692. PMID:26304272

Gleitman, H., Fridlund, A. J., & Reisberg, D. (1999). *Psychology* (5th ed.). New York: W. W. Norton.

Guo, D., Berry, M. W., Thompson, B. B., & Bailin, S. (2003). Knowledge-Enhanced Latent Semantic Indexing. *Information Retrieval*, *6*(2), 225–250. doi:10.1023/A:1023984205118

Kontostathis, A., & Pottenger, A. M. (2006). A framework for understanding Latent Semantic Indexing (LSI) performance. *Information Processing & Management*, *42*(1), 56–73. doi:10.1016/j.ipm.2004.11.007

Kornblith, H. (2006). Appeals to intuitions and the ambitions of epistemology. In S. Hetherington (Ed.), *Epistemology Futures*. Oxford University Press.

Landauer, T. K., Foltz, P. W., & Laham, D. (1998). An introduction to Latent Semantic Analysis. *Discourse Processes*, *25*(2-3), 259–284. doi:10.1080/01638539809545028

Miller, G. A. (1991). *The Science of Words*. Scientific American Library.

Overton, W. F. (2015). Taking Conceptual Analyses Seriously. *Research in Human Development*, *12*(3-4), 163–171. doi:10.1080/15427609.2015.1069158

Oxford Dictionary of Philosophy. (2005). 2nd ed.). Oxford University Press.

Sager, J. C. (2000). *Essays on Definition*. Amsterdam: Johns Benjamins Publishing. doi:10.1075/tlrp.4

Shalit, R. (2006). Meaning Equivalence Tests for Assessing Deep Comprehension of English Spatial Prepositions in College Students. Doctoral Dissertation. Department of Human Development and Applied Psychology, Ontario Institute for Studies in Education of University of Toronto.

Wiemer-Hastings, P. (1999). How Latent is Latent Semantic Analysis? In *Proceedings of the Sixteenth International Joint Conference on Artificial Intelligence* (pp. 932-937).

Wittgenstein, L. (1967). *Philosophical Investigations* (2nd ed.). (G. E. M. Anscombe, Trans.). Oxford: Basil Blackwell.

Related Readings

To continue IGI Global's long-standing tradition of advancing innovation through emerging research, please find below a compiled list of recommended IGI Global book chapters and journal articles in the areas of concept parsing, data storage, decentralized computing, and the internet of things. These related readings will provide additional information and guidance to further enrich your knowledge and assist you with your own research.

Abidi, N., Bandyopadhayay, A., & Gupta, V. (2017). Sustainable Supply Chain Management: A Three Dimensional Framework and Performance Metric for Indian IT Product Companies. [IJISSCM]. *International Journal of Information Systems and Supply Chain Management*, *10*(1), 29–52. doi:10.4018/IJISSCM.2017010103

Achahbar, O., & Abid, M. R. (2015). The Impact of Virtualization on High Performance Computing Clustering in the Cloud. [IJDST]. *International Journal of Distributed Systems and Technologies*, *6*(4), 65–81. doi:10.4018/IJDST.2015100104

Adhikari, M., Das, A., & Mukherjee, A. (2016). Utility Computing and Its Utilization. In G. Deka, G. Siddesh, K. Srinivasa, & L. Patnaik (Eds.), *Emerging Research Surrounding Power Consumption and Performance Issues in Utility Computing* (pp. 1–21). Hershey, PA: IGI Global; doi:10.4018/978-1-4666-8853-7.ch001

Aggarwal, S., & Nayak, A. (2016). Mobile Big Data: A New Frontier of Innovation. In J. Aguado, C. Feijóo, & I. Martínez (Eds.), *Emerging Perspectives on the Mobile Content Evolution* (pp. 138–158). Hershey, PA: IGI Global; doi:10.4018/978-1-4666-8838-4.ch008

Akherfi, K., Harroud, H., & Gerndt, M. (2016). A Mobile Cloud Middleware to Support Mobility and Cloud Interoperability. [IJARAS]. *International Journal of Adaptive, Resilient and Autonomic Systems, 7*(1), 41–58. doi:10.4018/IJARAS.2016010103

Al-Hamami, M. A. (2015). The Impact of Big Data on Security. In A. Al-Hamami & G. Waleed al-Saadoon (Eds.), *Handbook of Research on Threat Detection and Countermeasures in Network Security* (pp. 276–298). Hershey, PA: IGI Global; doi:10.4018/978-1-4666-6583-5.ch015

Al Jabri, H. A., Al-Badi, A. H., & Ali, O. (2017). Exploring the Usage of Big Data Analytical Tools in Telecommunication Industry in Oman. [IRMJ]. *Information Resources Management Journal, 30*(1), 1–14. doi:10.4018/IRMJ.2017010101

Alohali, B. (2016). Security in Cloud of Things (CoT). In Z. Ma (Ed.), *Managing Big Data in Cloud Computing Environments* (pp. 46–70). Hershey, PA: IGI Global; doi:10.4018/978-1-4666-9834-5.ch003

Alohali, B. (2017). Detection Protocol of Possible Crime Scenes Using Internet of Things (IoT). In M. Moore (Ed.), *Cybersecurity Breaches and Issues Surrounding Online Threat Protection* (pp. 175–196). Hershey, PA: IGI Global; doi:10.4018/978-1-5225-1941-6.ch008

AlZain, M. A., Li, A. S., Soh, B., & Pardede, E. (2015). Multi-Cloud Data Management using Shamirs Secret Sharing and Quantum Byzantine Agreement Schemes. [IJCAC]. *International Journal of Cloud Applications and Computing, 5*(3), 35–52. doi:10.4018/IJCAC.2015070103

Armstrong, S., & Yampolskiy, R. V. (2017). Security Solutions for Intelligent and Complex Systems. In M. Dawson, M. Eltayeb, & M. Omar (Eds.), *Security Solutions for Hyperconnectivity and the Internet of Things* (pp. 37–88). Hershey, PA: IGI Global; doi:10.4018/978-1-5225-0741-3.ch003

Attasena, V., Harbi, N., & Darmont, J. (2015). A Novel Multi-Secret Sharing Approach for Secure Data Warehousing and On-Line Analysis Processing in the Cloud. [IJDWM]. *International Journal of Data Warehousing and Mining, 11*(2), 22–43. doi:10.4018/ijdwm.2015040102

Awad, W. S., & Abdullah, H. M. (2014). Improving the Security of Storage Systems: Bahrain Case Study. [IJMCMC]. *International Journal of Mobile Computing and Multimedia Communications, 6*(3), 75–105. doi:10.4018/IJMCMC.2014070104

Bagui, S., & Nguyen, L. T. (2015). Database Sharding: To Provide Fault Tolerance and Scalability of Big Data on the Cloud. [IJCAC]. *International Journal of Cloud Applications and Computing, 5*(2), 36–52. doi:10.4018/IJCAC.2015040103

Barbierato, E., Gribaudo, M., & Iacono, M. (2016). Modeling and Evaluating the Effects of Big Data Storage Resource Allocation in Global Scale Cloud Architectures. [IJDWM]. *International Journal of Data Warehousing and Mining, 12*(2), 1–20. doi:10.4018/IJDWM.2016040101

Barbosa, J. L., Barbosa, D. N., Rigo, S. J., Machado de Oliveira, J., & Junior, S. A. (2017). Collaborative Learning on Decentralized Ubiquitous Environments. In L. Tomei (Ed.), *Exploring the New Era of Technology-Infused Education* (pp. 141–157). Hershey, PA: IGI Global; doi:10.4018/978-1-5225-1709-2.ch009

Benmounah, Z., Meshoul, S., & Batouche, M. (2017). Scalable Differential Evolutionary Clustering Algorithm for Big Data Using Map-Reduce Paradigm. [IJAMC]. *International Journal of Applied Metaheuristic Computing, 8*(1), 45–60. doi:10.4018/IJAMC.2017010103

Bhadoria, R. S. (2016). Performance of Enterprise Architecture in Utility Computing. In G. Deka, G. Siddesh, K. Srinivasa, & L. Patnaik (Eds.), *Emerging Research Surrounding Power Consumption and Performance Issues in Utility Computing* (pp. 44–68). Hershey, PA: IGI Global; doi:10.4018/978-1-4666-8853-7.ch003

Bhardwaj, A. (2017). Solutions for Securing End User Data over the Cloud Deployed Applications. In M. Moore (Ed.), *Cybersecurity Breaches and Issues Surrounding Online Threat Protection* (pp. 198–218). Hershey, PA: IGI Global; doi:10.4018/978-1-5225-1941-6.ch009

Bibi, S., Katsaros, D., & Bozanis, P. (2015). Cloud Computing Economics. In V. Díaz, J. Lovelle, & B. García-Bustelo (Eds.), *Handbook of Research on Innovations in Systems and Software Engineering* (pp. 125–149). Hershey, PA: IGI Global; doi:10.4018/978-1-4666-6359-6.ch005

Bihl, T. J., Young, W. A. II, & Weckman, G. R. (2016). Defining, Understanding, and Addressing Big Data. [IJBAN]. *International Journal of Business Analytics, 3*(2), 1–32. doi:10.4018/IJBAN.2016040101

Bimonte, S., Sautot, L., Journaux, L., & Faivre, B. (2017). Multidimensional Model Design using Data Mining: A Rapid Prototyping Methodology. [IJDWM]. *International Journal of Data Warehousing and Mining, 13*(1), 1–35. doi:10.4018/IJDWM.2017010101

Bruno, G. (2017). A Dataflow-Oriented Modeling Approach to Business Processes. [IJHCITP]. *International Journal of Human Capital and Information Technology Professionals, 8*(1), 51–65. doi:10.4018/IJHCITP.2017010104

Chande, S. V. (2014). Cloud Database Systems: NoSQL, NewSQL, and Hybrid. In P. Raj & G. Deka (Eds.), *Handbook of Research on Cloud Infrastructures for Big Data Analytics* (pp. 216–231). Hershey, PA: IGI Global; doi:10.4018/978-1-4666-5864-6.ch009

Copie, A. Manațe, B., Munteanu, V. I., & Fortiş, T. (2015). An Internet of Things Governance Architecture with Applications in Healthcare. In F. Xhafa, P. Moore, & G. Tadros (Eds.), Advanced Technological Solutions for E-Health and Dementia Patient Monitoring (pp. 322-344). Hershey, PA: IGI Global. doi:10.4018/978-1-4666-7481-3.ch013

Cordeschi, N., Shojafar, M., Amendola, D., & Baccarelli, E. (2015). Energy-Saving QoS Resource Management of Virtualized Networked Data Centers for Big Data Stream Computing. In S. Bagchi (Ed.), *Emerging Research in Cloud Distributed Computing Systems* (pp. 122–155). Hershey, PA: IGI Global; doi:10.4018/978-1-4666-8213-9.ch004

Costan, A. A., Iancu, B., Rasa, P. C., Radu, A., Peculea, A., & Dadarlat, V. T. (2017). Intercloud: Delivering Innovative Cloud Services. In I. Hosu & I. Iancu (Eds.), *Digital Entrepreneurship and Global Innovation* (pp. 59–78). Hershey, PA: IGI Global; doi:10.4018/978-1-5225-0953-0.ch004

Croatti, A., Ricci, A., & Viroli, M. (2017). Towards a Mobile Augmented Reality System for Emergency Management: The Case of SAFE. [IJDST]. *International Journal of Distributed Systems and Technologies, 8*(1), 46–58. doi:10.4018/IJDST.2017010104

David-West, O. (2016). Information and Communications Technology (ICT) and the Supply Chain. In B. Christiansen (Ed.), *Handbook of Research on Global Supply Chain Management* (pp. 495–515). Hershey, PA: IGI Global; doi:10.4018/978-1-4666-9639-6.ch028

Dawson, M. (2017). Exploring Secure Computing for the Internet of Things, Internet of Everything, Web of Things, and Hyperconnectivity. In M. Dawson, M. Eltayeb, & M. Omar (Eds.), *Security Solutions for Hyperconnectivity and the Internet of Things* (pp. 1–12). Hershey, PA: IGI Global; doi:10.4018/978-1-5225-0741-3.ch001

Delgado, J. C. (2015). An Interoperability Framework for Enterprise Applications in Cloud Environments. In N. Rao (Ed.), *Enterprise Management Strategies in the Era of Cloud Computing* (pp. 26–59). Hershey, PA: IGI Global; doi:10.4018/978-1-4666-8339-6.ch002

Dhal, S. K., Verma, H., & Addya, S. K. (2017). Resource and Energy Efficient Virtual Machine Migration in Cloud Data Centers. In A. Turuk, B. Sahoo, & S. Addya (Eds.), *Resource Management and Efficiency in Cloud Computing Environments* (pp. 210–238). Hershey, PA: IGI Global; doi:10.4018/978-1-5225-1721-4.ch009

Duggirala, S. (2014). Big Data Architecture: Storage and Computation. In P. Raj & G. Deka (Eds.), *Handbook of Research on Cloud Infrastructures for Big Data Analytics* (pp. 129–156). Hershey, PA: IGI Global; doi:10.4018/978-1-4666-5864-6.ch006

Easton, J., & Parmar, R. (2017). Navigating Your Way to the Hybrid Cloud. In J. Chen, Y. Zhang, & R. Gottschalk (Eds.), *Handbook of Research on End-to-End Cloud Computing Architecture Design* (pp. 15–38). Hershey, PA: IGI Global; doi:10.4018/978-1-5225-0759-8.ch002

Elkabbany, G. F., & Rasslan, M. (2017). Security Issues in Distributed Computing System Models. In M. Dawson, M. Eltayeb, & M. Omar (Eds.), *Security Solutions for Hyperconnectivity and the Internet of Things* (pp. 211–259). Hershey, PA: IGI Global; doi:10.4018/978-1-5225-0741-3.ch009

Elkhodr, M., Shahrestani, S., & Cheung, H. (2016). Wireless Enabling Technologies for the Internet of Things. In Q. Hassan (Ed.), *Innovative Research and Applications in Next-Generation High Performance Computing* (pp. 368–396). Hershey, PA: IGI Global; doi:10.4018/978-1-5225-0287-6.ch015

Elkhodr, M., Shahrestani, S., & Cheung, H. (2017). Internet of Things Research Challenges. In M. Dawson, M. Eltayeb, & M. Omar (Eds.), *Security Solutions for Hyperconnectivity and the Internet of Things* (pp. 13–36). Hershey, PA: IGI Global; doi:10.4018/978-1-5225-0741-3.ch002

Erturk, E. (2017). Cloud Computing and Cybersecurity Issues Facing Local Enterprises. In M. Moore (Ed.), *Cybersecurity Breaches and Issues Surrounding Online Threat Protection* (pp. 219–247). Hershey, PA: IGI Global; doi:10.4018/978-1-5225-1941-6.ch010

Ferreira da Silva, R., Glatard, T., & Desprez, F. (2015). Self-Management of Operational Issues for Grid Computing: The Case of the Virtual Imaging Platform. In S. Bagchi (Ed.), *Emerging Research in Cloud Distributed Computing Systems* (pp. 187–221). Hershey, PA: IGI Global; doi:10.4018/978-1-4666-8213-9.ch006

Fu, S., He, L., Liao, X., Huang, C., Li, K., & Chang, C. (2015). Analyzing and Boosting the Data Availability in Decentralized Online Social Networks. [IJWSR]. *International Journal of Web Services Research, 12*(2), 47–72. doi:10.4018/IJWSR.2015040103

Gao, F., & Zhao, Q. (2014). Big Data Based Logistics Data Mining Platform: Architecture and Implementation. [IJITN]. *International Journal of Interdisciplinary Telecommunications and Networking, 6*(4), 24–34. doi:10.4018/IJITN.2014100103

Gudivada, V. N., Nandigam, J., & Paris, J. (2015). Programming Paradigms in High Performance Computing. In R. Segall, J. Cook, & Q. Zhang (Eds.), *Research and Applications in Global Supercomputing* (pp. 303–330). Hershey, PA: IGI Global; doi:10.4018/978-1-4666-7461-5.ch013

Hagos, D. H. (2016). Software-Defined Networking for Scalable Cloud-based Services to Improve System Performance of Hadoop-based Big Data Applications. [IJGHPC]. *International Journal of Grid and High Performance Computing, 8*(2), 1–22. doi:10.4018/IJGHPC.2016040101

Hallappanavar, V. L., & Birje, M. N. (2017). Trust Management in Cloud Computing. In M. Dawson, M. Eltayeb, & M. Omar (Eds.), *Security Solutions for Hyperconnectivity and the Internet of Things* (pp. 151–183). Hershey, PA: IGI Global; doi:10.4018/978-1-5225-0741-3.ch007

Hameur Laine, A., & Brahimi, S. (2017). Background on Context-Aware Computing Systems. In C. Reis & M. Maximiano (Eds.), *Internet of Things and Advanced Application in Healthcare* (pp. 1–31). Hershey, PA: IGI Global; doi:10.4018/978-1-5225-1820-4.ch001

Hamidi, H. (2017). A Model for Impact of Organizational Project Benefits Management and its Impact on End User. [JOEUC]. *Journal of Organizational and End User Computing, 29*(1), 51–65. doi:10.4018/JOEUC.2017010104

Hamidine, H., & Mahmood, A. (2017). Cloud Computing Data Storage Security Based on Different Encryption Schemes. In J. Chen, Y. Zhang, & R. Gottschalk (Eds.), *Handbook of Research on End-to-End Cloud Computing Architecture Design* (pp. 189–221). Hershey, PA: IGI Global; doi:10.4018/978-1-5225-0759-8.ch009

Hamidine, H., & Mahmood, A. (2017). Cloud Computing Data Storage Security Based on Different Encryption Schemes. In J. Chen, Y. Zhang, & R. Gottschalk (Eds.), *Handbook of Research on End-to-End Cloud Computing Architecture Design* (pp. 189–221). Hershey, PA: IGI Global; doi:10.4018/978-1-5225-0759-8.ch009

Hao, Y., & Helo, P. (2015). Cloud Manufacturing towards Sustainable Management. In F. Soliman (Ed.), *Business Transformation and Sustainability through Cloud System Implementation* (pp. 121–139). Hershey, PA: IGI Global; doi:10.4018/978-1-4666-6445-6.ch009

Hasan, N., & Rahman, A. A. (2017). Ranking the Factors that Impact Customers Online Participation in Value Co-creation in Service Sector Using Analytic Hierarchy Process. [IJISSS]. *International Journal of Information Systems in the Service Sector, 9*(1), 37–53. doi:10.4018/IJISSS.2017010103

Hashemi, S., Monfaredi, K., & Hashemi, S. Y. (2015). Cloud Computing for Secure Services in E-Government Architecture. [JITR]. *Journal of Information Technology Research, 8*(1), 43–61. doi:10.4018/JITR.2015010104

Hayajneh, S. M. (2015). Cloud Computing SaaS Paradigm for Efficient Modelling of Solar Features and Activities. [IJCAC]. *International Journal of Cloud Applications and Computing, 5*(3), 20–34. doi:10.4018/IJCAC.2015070102

Huang, L. K. (2017). A Cultural Model of Online Banking Adoption: Long-Term Orientation Perspective. [JOEUC]. *Journal of Organizational and End User Computing, 29*(1), 1–22. doi:10.4018/JOEUC.2017010101

Jacob, G., & Annamalai, M. (2017). Secure Storage and Transmission of Healthcare Records. In V. Tiwari, B. Tiwari, R. Thakur, & S. Gupta (Eds.), *Pattern and Data Analysis in Healthcare Settings* (pp. 7–34). Hershey, PA: IGI Global; doi:10.4018/978-1-5225-0536-5.ch002

Jadon, K. S., Mudgal, P., & Bhadoria, R. S. (2016). Optimization and Management of Resource in Utility Computing. In G. Deka, G. Siddesh, K. Srinivasa, & L. Patnaik (Eds.), *Emerging Research Surrounding Power Consumption and Performance Issues in Utility Computing* (pp. 22–43). Hershey, PA: IGI Global; doi:10.4018/978-1-4666-8853-7.ch002

Jararweh, Y., Al-Sharqawi, O., Abdulla, N., Tawalbeh, L., & Alhammouri, M. (2014). High-Throughput Encryption for Cloud Computing Storage System. [IJCAC]. *International Journal of Cloud Applications and Computing*, 4(2), 1–14. doi:10.4018/ijcac.2014040101

Jha, M., Jha, S., & O'Brien, L. (2017). Social Media and Big Data: A Conceptual Foundation for Organizations. In R. Chugh (Ed.), *Harnessing Social Media as a Knowledge Management Tool* (pp. 315–332). Hershey, PA: IGI Global; doi:10.4018/978-1-5225-0495-5.ch015

Kantarci, B., & Mouftah, H. T. (2015). Sensing as a Service in Cloud-Centric Internet of Things Architecture. In T. Soyata (Ed.), *Enabling Real-Time Mobile Cloud Computing through Emerging Technologies* (pp. 83–115). Hershey, PA: IGI Global; doi:10.4018/978-1-4666-8662-5.ch003

Kasemsap, K. (2015). The Role of Cloud Computing Adoption in Global Business. In V. Chang, R. Walters, & G. Wills (Eds.), *Delivery and Adoption of Cloud Computing Services in Contemporary Organizations* (pp. 26–55). Hershey, PA: IGI Global; doi:10.4018/978-1-4666-8210-8.ch002

Kasemsap, K. (2015). The Role of Cloud Computing in Global Supply Chain. In N. Rao (Ed.), *Enterprise Management Strategies in the Era of Cloud Computing* (pp. 192–219). Hershey, PA: IGI Global; doi:10.4018/978-1-4666-8339-6.ch009

Kasemsap, K. (2017). Mastering Intelligent Decision Support Systems in Enterprise Information Management. In G. Sreedhar (Ed.), *Web Data Mining and the Development of Knowledge-Based Decision Support Systems* (pp. 35–56). Hershey, PA: IGI Global; doi:10.4018/978-1-5225-1877-8.ch004

Kaukalias, T., & Chatzimisios, P. (2015). Internet of Things (IoT). In M. Khosrow-Pour (Ed.), *Encyclopedia of Information Science and Technology* (3rd ed., pp. 7623–7632). Hershey, PA: IGI Global; doi:10.4018/978-1-4666-5888-2.ch751

Kavoura, A., & Koziol, L. (2017). Polish Firms' Innovation Capability for Competitiveness via Information Technologies and Social Media Implementation. In A. Vlachvei, O. Notta, K. Karantininis, & N. Tsounis (Eds.), *Factors Affecting Firm Competitiveness and Performance in the Modern Business World* (pp. 191–222). Hershey, PA: IGI Global; doi:10.4018/978-1-5225-0843-4.ch007

Khan, I. U., Hameed, Z., & Khan, S. U. (2017). Understanding Online Banking Adoption in a Developing Country: UTAUT2 with Cultural Moderators. [JGIM]. *Journal of Global Information Management*, *25*(1), 43–65. doi:10.4018/JGIM.2017010103

Kirci, P. (2017). Ubiquitous and Cloud Computing: Ubiquitous Computing. In A. Turuk, B. Sahoo, & S. Addya (Eds.), *Resource Management and Efficiency in Cloud Computing Environments* (pp. 1–32). Hershey, PA: IGI Global; doi:10.4018/978-1-5225-1721-4.ch001

Kofahi, I., & Alryalat, H. (2017). Enterprise Resource Planning (ERP) Implementation Approaches and the Performance of Procure-to-Pay Business Processes: (Field Study in Companies that Implement Oracle ERP in Jordan). [IJITPM]. *International Journal of Information Technology Project Management*, *8*(1), 55–71. doi:10.4018/IJITPM.2017010104

Koumaras, H., Damaskos, C., Diakoumakos, G., Kourtis, M., Xilouris, G., Gardikis, G., & Siakoulis, T. et al. (2015). Virtualization Evolution: From IT Infrastructure Abstraction of Cloud Computing to Virtualization of Network Functions. In G. Mastorakis, C. Mavromoustakis, & E. Pallis (Eds.), *Resource Management of Mobile Cloud Computing Networks and Environments* (pp. 279–306). Hershey, PA: IGI Global; doi:10.4018/978-1-4666-8225-2.ch010

Kuada, E. (2017). Security and Trust in Cloud Computing. In M. Dawson, M. Eltayeb, & M. Omar (Eds.), *Security Solutions for Hyperconnectivity and the Internet of Things* (pp. 184–210). Hershey, PA: IGI Global; doi:10.4018/978-1-5225-0741-3.ch008

Kumar, D., Sahoo, B., & Mandal, T. (2015). Heuristic Task Consolidation Techniques for Energy Efficient Cloud Computing. In N. Rao (Ed.), *Enterprise Management Strategies in the Era of Cloud Computing* (pp. 238–260). Hershey, PA: IGI Global; doi:10.4018/978-1-4666-8339-6.ch011

Lee, C. K., Cao, Y., & Ng, K. H. (2017). Big Data Analytics for Predictive Maintenance Strategies. In H. Chan, N. Subramanian, & M. Abdulrahman (Eds.), *Supply Chain Management in the Big Data Era* (pp. 50–74). Hershey, PA: IGI Global; doi:10.4018/978-1-5225-0956-1.ch004

Liao, W. (2016). Application of Hadoop in the Document Storage Management System for Telecommunication Enterprise. [IJITN]. *International Journal of Interdisciplinary Telecommunications and Networking*, 8(2), 58–68. doi:10.4018/IJITN.2016040106

Liew, C. S., Ang, J. M., Goh, Y. T., Koh, W. K., Tan, S. Y., & Teh, R. Y. (2017). Factors Influencing Consumer Acceptance of Internet of Things Technology. In N. Suki (Ed.), *Handbook of Research on Leveraging Consumer Psychology for Effective Customer Engagement* (pp. 186–201). Hershey, PA: IGI Global; doi:10.4018/978-1-5225-0746-8.ch012

Lytras, M. D., Raghavan, V., & Damiani, E. (2017). Big Data and Data Analytics Research: From Metaphors to Value Space for Collective Wisdom in Human Decision Making and Smart Machines. [IJSWIS]. *International Journal on Semantic Web and Information Systems*, 13(1), 1–10. doi:10.4018/IJSWIS.2017010101

Mabe, L. K., & Oladele, O. I. (2017). Application of Information Communication Technologies for Agricultural Development through Extension Services: A Review. In T. Tossy (Ed.), *Information Technology Integration for Socio-Economic Development* (pp. 52–101). Hershey, PA: IGI Global; doi:10.4018/978-1-5225-0539-6.ch003

Machaka, P., & Nelwamondo, F. (2016). Data Mining Techniques for Distributed Denial of Service Attacks Detection in the Internet of Things: A Research Survey. In O. Isafiade & A. Bagula (Eds.), *Data Mining Trends and Applications in Criminal Science and Investigations* (pp. 275–334). Hershey, PA: IGI Global; doi:10.4018/978-1-5225-0463-4.ch010

Manohari, P. K., & Ray, N. K. (2017). A Comprehensive Study of Security in Cloud Computing. In N. Ray & A. Turuk (Eds.), *Handbook of Research on Advanced Wireless Sensor Network Applications, Protocols, and Architectures* (pp. 386–412). Hershey, PA: IGI Global; doi:10.4018/978-1-5225-0486-3.ch016

Manvi, S. S., & Hegde, N. (2017). Vehicular Cloud Computing Challenges and Security. In S. Bhattacharyya, N. Das, D. Bhattacharjee, & A. Mukherjee (Eds.), *Handbook of Research on Recent Developments in Intelligent Communication Application* (pp. 344–365). Hershey, PA: IGI Global; doi:10.4018/978-1-5225-1785-6.ch013

McKelvey, N., Curran, K., & Subaginy, N. (2015). The Internet of Things. In M. Khosrow-Pour (Ed.), *Encyclopedia of Information Science and Technology* (3rd ed., pp. 5777–5783). Hershey, PA: IGI Global; doi:10.4018/978-1-4666-5888-2.ch570

Meddah, I. H., Belkadi, K., & Boudia, M. A. (2017). Efficient Implementation of Hadoop MapReduce based Business Process Dataflow. [IJDSST]. *International Journal of Decision Support System Technology*, *9*(1), 49–60. doi:10.4018/IJDSST.2017010104

Meghanathan, N. (2015). Virtualization as the Catalyst for Cloud Computing. In M. Khosrow-Pour (Ed.), *Encyclopedia of Information Science and Technology* (3rd ed., pp. 1096–1110). Hershey, PA: IGI Global; doi:10.4018/978-1-4666-5888-2.ch105

Mehenni, T. (2017). Geographic Knowledge Discovery in Multiple Spatial Databases. In S. Faiz & K. Mahmoudi (Eds.), *Handbook of Research on Geographic Information Systems Applications and Advancements* (pp. 344–366). Hershey, PA: IGI Global; doi:10.4018/978-1-5225-0937-0.ch013

Mehrotra, S., & Kohli, S. (2017). Data Clustering and Various Clustering Approaches. In S. Bhattacharyya, S. De, I. Pan, & P. Dutta (Eds.), *Intelligent Multidimensional Data Clustering and Analysis* (pp. 90–108). Hershey, PA: IGI Global; doi:10.4018/978-1-5225-1776-4.ch004

Meralto, C., Moura, J., & Marinheiro, R. (2017). Wireless Mesh Sensor Networks with Mobile Devices: A Comprehensive Review. In N. Ray & A. Turuk (Eds.), *Handbook of Research on Advanced Wireless Sensor Network Applications, Protocols, and Architectures* (pp. 129–155). Hershey, PA: IGI Global; doi:10.4018/978-1-5225-0486-3.ch005

Moradbeikie, A., Abrishami, S., & Abbasi, H. (2016). Creating Time-Limited Attributes for Time-Limited Services in Cloud Computing. [IJISP]. *International Journal of Information Security and Privacy*, *10*(4), 44–57. doi:10.4018/IJISP.2016100103

Mourtzoukos, K., Kefalakis, N., & Soldatos, J. (2015). Open Source Object Directory Services for Inter-Enterprise Tracking and Tracing Applications. In I. Lee (Ed.), *RFID Technology Integration for Business Performance Improvement* (pp. 80–97). Hershey, PA: IGI Global; doi:10.4018/978-1-4666-6308-4.ch004

Mugisha, E., Zhang, G., El Abidine, M. Z., & Eugene, M. (2017). A TPM-based Secure Multi-Cloud Storage Architecture grounded on Erasure Codes. [IJISP]. *International Journal of Information Security and Privacy*, *11*(1), 52–64. doi:10.4018/IJISP.2017010104

Munir, K. (2017). Security Model for Mobile Cloud Database as a Service (DBaaS). In K. Munir (Ed.), *Security Management in Mobile Cloud Computing* (pp. 169–180). Hershey, PA: IGI Global; doi:10.4018/978-1-5225-0602-7.ch008

Murugaiyan, S. R., Chandramohan, D., Vengattaraman, T., & Dhavachelvan, P. (2014). A Generic Privacy Breach Preventing Methodology for Cloud Based Web Service. [IJGHPC]. *International Journal of Grid and High Performance Computing*, *6*(3), 53–84. doi:10.4018/ijghpc.2014070104

Naeem, M. A., & Jamil, N. (2015). Online Processing of End-User Data in Real-Time Data Warehousing. In M. Usman (Ed.), *Improving Knowledge Discovery through the Integration of Data Mining Techniques* (pp. 13–31). Hershey, PA: IGI Global; doi:10.4018/978-1-4666-8513-0.ch002

Nayak, P. (2017). Internet of Things Services, Applications, Issues, and Challenges. In N. Ray & A. Turuk (Eds.), *Handbook of Research on Advanced Wireless Sensor Network Applications, Protocols, and Architectures* (pp. 353–368). Hershey, PA: IGI Global; doi:10.4018/978-1-5225-0486-3.ch014

Nekaj, E. L. (2017). The Crowd Economy: From the Crowd to Businesses to Public Administrations and Multinational Companies. In W. Vassallo (Ed.), *Crowdfunding for Sustainable Entrepreneurship and Innovation* (pp. 1–19). Hershey, PA: IGI Global; doi:10.4018/978-1-5225-0568-6.ch001

Omar, M. (2015). Cloud Computing Security: Abuse and Nefarious Use of Cloud Computing. In K. Munir, M. Al-Mutairi, & L. Mohammed (Eds.), *Handbook of Research on Security Considerations in Cloud Computing* (pp. 30–38). Hershey, PA: IGI Global; doi:10.4018/978-1-4666-8387-7.ch002

Orike, S., & Brown, D. (2016). Big Data Management: An Investigation into Wireless and Cloud Computing. [IJITN]. *International Journal of Interdisciplinary Telecommunications and Networking*, 8(4), 34–50. doi:10.4018/IJITN.2016100104

Ouf, S., & Nasr, M. (2015). Cloud Computing: The Future of Big Data Management. [IJCAC]. *International Journal of Cloud Applications and Computing*, 5(2), 53–61. doi:10.4018/IJCAC.2015040104

Ozpinar, A., & Yarkan, S. (2016). Vehicle to Cloud: Big Data for Environmental Sustainability, Energy, and Traffic Management. In M. Singh, & D. G. (Eds.), Effective Big Data Management and Opportunities for Implementation (pp. 182-201). Hershey, PA: IGI Global. doi:10.4018/978-1-5225-0182-4.ch012

Pal, A., & Kumar, M. (2017). Collaborative Filtering Based Data Mining for Large Data. In V. Bhatnagar (Ed.), *Collaborative Filtering Using Data Mining and Analysis* (pp. 115–127). Hershey, PA: IGI Global; doi:10.4018/978-1-5225-0489-4.ch006

Pal, K., & Karakostas, B. (2016). A Game-Based Approach for Simulation and Design of Supply Chains. In T. Kramberger, V. Potočan, & V. Ipavec (Eds.), *Sustainable Logistics and Strategic Transportation Planning* (pp. 1–23). Hershey, PA: IGI Global; doi:10.4018/978-1-5225-0001-8.ch001

Panda, S. (2017). Security Issues and Challenges in Internet of Things. In N. Ray & A. Turuk (Eds.), *Handbook of Research on Advanced Wireless Sensor Network Applications, Protocols, and Architectures* (pp. 369–385). Hershey, PA: IGI Global; doi:10.4018/978-1-5225-0486-3.ch015

Pandit, S., Milman, I., Oberhofer, M., & Zhou, Y. (2017). Principled Reference Data Management for Big Data and Business Intelligence. [IJOCI]. *International Journal of Organizational and Collective Intelligence*, 7(1), 47–66. doi:10.4018/IJOCI.2017010104

Paul, A. K., & Sahoo, B. (2017). Dynamic Virtual Machine Placement in Cloud Computing. In A. Turuk, B. Sahoo, & S. Addya (Eds.), *Resource Management and Efficiency in Cloud Computing Environments* (pp. 136–167). Hershey, PA: IGI Global; doi:10.4018/978-1-5225-1721-4.ch006

Petri, I., Diaz-Montes, J., Zou, M., Zamani, A. R., Beach, T. H., Rana, O. F., & Rezgui, Y. et al. (2016). Distributed Multi-Cloud Based Building Data Analytics. In G. Kecskemeti, A. Kertesz, & Z. Nemeth (Eds.), *Developing Interoperable and Federated Cloud Architecture* (pp. 143–169). Hershey, PA: IGI Global; doi:10.4018/978-1-5225-0153-4.ch006

Poleto, T., Heuer de Carvalho, V. D., & Costa, A. P. (2017). The Full Knowledge of Big Data in the Integration of Inter-Organizational Information: An Approach Focused on Decision Making. [IJDSST]. *International Journal of Decision Support System Technology*, 9(1), 16–31. doi:10.4018/ IJDSST.2017010102

Rahman, N., & Iverson, S. (2015). Big Data Business Intelligence in Bank Risk Analysis. [IJBIR]. *International Journal of Business Intelligence Research*, 6(2), 55–77. doi:10.4018/IJBIR.2015070104

Raj, P. (2014). Big Data Analytics Demystified. In P. Raj & G. Deka (Eds.), *Handbook of Research on Cloud Infrastructures for Big Data Analytics* (pp. 38–73). Hershey, PA: IGI Global; doi:10.4018/978-1-4666-5864-6.ch003

Raj, P. (2014). The Compute Infrastructures for Big Data Analytics. In P. Raj & G. Deka (Eds.), *Handbook of Research on Cloud Infrastructures for Big Data Analytics* (pp. 74–109). Hershey, PA: IGI Global; doi:10.4018/978-1-4666-5864-6.ch004

Raj, P. (2014). The Network Infrastructures for Big Data Analytics. In P. Raj & G. Deka (Eds.), *Handbook of Research on Cloud Infrastructures for Big Data Analytics* (pp. 157–185). Hershey, PA: IGI Global; doi:10.4018/978-1-4666-5864-6.ch007

Raman, A. C. (2014). Storage Infrastructure for Big Data and Cloud. In P. Raj & G. Deka (Eds.), *Handbook of Research on Cloud Infrastructures for Big Data Analytics* (pp. 110–128). Hershey, PA: IGI Global; doi:10.4018/978-1-4666-5864-6.ch005

Rao, A. P. (2017). Discovering Knowledge Hidden in Big Data from Machine-Learning Techniques. In G. Sreedhar (Ed.), *Web Data Mining and the Development of Knowledge-Based Decision Support Systems* (pp. 167–183). Hershey, PA: IGI Global; doi:10.4018/978-1-5225-1877-8.ch010

Rathore, M. M., Paul, A., Ahmad, A., & Jeon, G. (2017). IoT-Based Big Data: From Smart City towards Next Generation Super City Planning. [IJSWIS]. *International Journal on Semantic Web and Information Systems*, *13*(1), 28–47. doi:10.4018/IJSWIS.2017010103

Ratten, V. (2015). An Entrepreneurial Approach to Cloud Computing Design and Application: Technological Innovation and Information System Usage. In S. Aljawarneh (Ed.), *Advanced Research on Cloud Computing Design and Applications* (pp. 1–14). Hershey, PA: IGI Global; doi:10.4018/978-1-4666-8676-2.ch001

Rebekah, R. D., Cheelu, D., & Babu, M. R. (2017). Necessity of Key Aggregation Cryptosystem for Data Sharing in Cloud Computing. In P. Krishna (Ed.), *Emerging Technologies and Applications for Cloud-Based Gaming* (pp. 210–227). Hershey, PA: IGI Global; doi:10.4018/978-1-5225-0546-4.ch010

Rehman, A., Ullah, R., & Abdullah, F. (2015). Big Data Analysis in IoT. In N. Zaman, M. Seliaman, M. Hassan, & F. Marquez (Eds.), *Handbook of Research on Trends and Future Directions in Big Data and Web Intelligence* (pp. 313–327). Hershey, PA: IGI Global; doi:10.4018/978-1-4666-8505-5. ch015

Rehman, M. H., Khan, A. U., & Batool, A. (2016). Big Data Analytics in Mobile and Cloud Computing Environments. In Q. Hassan (Ed.), *Innovative Research and Applications in Next-Generation High Performance Computing* (pp. 349–367). Hershey, PA: IGI Global; doi:10.4018/978-1-5225-0287-6. ch014

Rosado da Cruz, A. M., & Paiva, S. (2016). Cloud and Mobile: A Future Together. In A. Rosado da Cruz & S. Paiva (Eds.), *Modern Software Engineering Methodologies for Mobile and Cloud Environments* (pp. 1–20). Hershey, PA: IGI Global; doi:10.4018/978-1-4666-9916-8.ch001

Rusko, R. (2017). Strategic Turning Points in ICT Business: The Business Development, Transformation, and Evolution in the Case of Nokia. In I. Oncioiu (Ed.), *Driving Innovation and Business Success in the Digital Economy* (pp. 1–15). Hershey, PA: IGI Global; doi:10.4018/978-1-5225-1779-5.ch001

Sahlin, J. P. (2015). Federal Government Application of the Cloud Computing Application Integration Model. In M. Khosrow-Pour (Ed.), *Encyclopedia of Information Science and Technology* (3rd ed., pp. 2735–2744). Hershey, PA: IGI Global; doi:10.4018/978-1-4666-5888-2.ch267

Sahoo, S., Sahoo, B., Turuk, A. K., & Mishra, S. K. (2017). Real Time Task Execution in Cloud Using MapReduce Framework. In A. Turuk, B. Sahoo, & S. Addya (Eds.), *Resource Management and Efficiency in Cloud Computing Environments* (pp. 190–209). Hershey, PA: IGI Global; doi:10.4018/978-1-5225-1721-4.ch008

Schnjakin, M., & Meinel, C. (2014). Solving Security and Availability Challenges in Public Clouds. In A. Kayem & C. Meinel (Eds.), *Information Security in Diverse Computing Environments* (pp. 280–302). Hershey, PA: IGI Global; doi:10.4018/978-1-4666-6158-5.ch015

Shaikh, F. (2017). The Benefits of New Online (Digital) Technologies on Business: Understanding the Impact of Digital on Different Aspects of the Business. In I. Hosu & I. Iancu (Eds.), *Digital Entrepreneurship and Global Innovation* (pp. 1–17). Hershey, PA: IGI Global; doi:10.4018/978-1-5225-0953-0.ch001

Shalan, M. (2017). Cloud Service Footprint (CSF): Utilizing Risk and Governance Directions to Characterize a Cloud Service. In A. Turuk, B. Sahoo, & S. Addya (Eds.), *Resource Management and Efficiency in Cloud Computing Environments* (pp. 61–88). Hershey, PA: IGI Global; doi:10.4018/978-1-5225-1721-4.ch003

Sharma, A., & Tandekar, P. (2017). Cyber Security and Business Growth. In Rajagopal, & R. Behl (Eds.), Business Analytics and Cyber Security Management in Organizations (pp. 14-27). Hershey, PA: IGI Global. doi:10.4018/978-1-5225-0902-8.ch002

Shen, Y., Li, Y., Wu, L., Liu, S., & Wen, Q. (2014). Big Data Techniques, Tools, and Applications. In Y. Shen, Y. Li, L. Wu, S. Liu, & Q. Wen (Eds.), *Enabling the New Era of Cloud Computing: Data Security, Transfer, and Management* (pp. 185–212). Hershey, PA: IGI Global; doi:10.4018/978-1-4666-4801-2.ch009

Shen, Y., Li, Y., Wu, L., Liu, S., & Wen, Q. (2014). Cloud Infrastructure: Virtualization. In Y. Shen, Y. Li, L. Wu, S. Liu, & Q. Wen (Eds.), *Enabling the New Era of Cloud Computing: Data Security, Transfer, and Management* (pp. 51–76). Hershey, PA: IGI Global; doi:10.4018/978-1-4666-4801-2.ch003

Siddesh, G. M., Srinivasa, K. G., & Tejaswini, L. (2015). Recent Trends in Cloud Computing Security Issues and Their Mitigation. In G. Deka & S. Bakshi (Eds.), *Handbook of Research on Securing Cloud-Based Databases with Biometric Applications* (pp. 16–46). Hershey, PA: IGI Global; doi:10.4018/978-1-4666-6559-0.ch002

Singh, B., & K.S., J. (2017). Security Management in Mobile Cloud Computing: Security and Privacy Issues and Solutions in Mobile Cloud Computing. In K. Munir (Ed.), *Security Management in Mobile Cloud Computing* (pp. 148-168). Hershey, PA: IGI Global. doi:10.4018/978-1-5225-0602-7.ch007

Singh, J., Gimekar, A. M., & Venkatesan, S. (2017). An Overview of Big Data Security with Hadoop Framework. In M. Kumar (Ed.), *Applied Big Data Analytics in Operations Management* (pp. 165–181). Hershey, PA: IGI Global; doi:10.4018/978-1-5225-0886-1.ch008

Singh, S., & Singh, J. (2017). Management of SME's Semi Structured Data Using Semantic Technique. In M. Kumar (Ed.), *Applied Big Data Analytics in Operations Management* (pp. 133–164). Hershey, PA: IGI Global; doi:10.4018/978-1-5225-0886-1.ch007

Sokolowski, L., & Oussena, S. (2016). Using Big Data in Collaborative Learning. In M. Atzmueller, S. Oussena, & T. Roth-Berghofer (Eds.), *Enterprise Big Data Engineering, Analytics, and Management* (pp. 221–237). Hershey, PA: IGI Global; doi:10.4018/978-1-5225-0293-7.ch013

Soliman, F. (2015). Evaluation of Cloud System Success Factors in Supply-Demand Chains. In F. Soliman (Ed.), *Business Transformation and Sustainability through Cloud System Implementation* (pp. 90–104). Hershey, PA: IGI Global; doi:10.4018/978-1-4666-6445-6.ch007

Srinivasan, S. (2014). Meeting Compliance Requirements while using Cloud Services. In S. Srinivasan (Ed.), *Security, Trust, and Regulatory Aspects of Cloud Computing in Business Environments* (pp. 127–144). Hershey, PA: IGI Global; doi:10.4018/978-1-4666-5788-5.ch007

Sun, X., & Wei, Z. (2015). The Dynamic Data Privacy Protection Strategy Based on the CAP Theory. [IJITN]. *International Journal of Interdisciplinary Telecommunications and Networking*, 7(1), 44–56. doi:10.4018/ijitn.2015010104

Sundararajan, S., Bhasi, M., & Pramod, K. (2017). Managing Software Risks in Maintenance Projects, from a Vendor Perspective: A Case Study in Global Software Development. [IJITPM]. *International Journal of Information Technology Project Management*, 8(1), 35–54. doi:10.4018/IJITPM.2017010103

Sundaresan, M., & Boopathy, D. (2014). Different Perspectives of Cloud Security. In S. Srinivasan (Ed.), *Security, Trust, and Regulatory Aspects of Cloud Computing in Business Environments* (pp. 73–90). Hershey, PA: IGI Global; doi:10.4018/978-1-4666-5788-5.ch004

Sutagundar, A. V., & Hatti, D. (2017). Data Management in Internet of Things. In N. Kamila (Ed.), *Handbook of Research on Wireless Sensor Network Trends, Technologies, and Applications* (pp. 80–97). Hershey, PA: IGI Global; doi:10.4018/978-1-5225-0501-3.ch004

Swacha, J. (2014). Measuring and Managing the Economics of Information Storage. In T. Tsiakis, T. Kargidis, & P. Katsaros (Eds.), *Approaches and Processes for Managing the Economics of Information Systems* (pp. 47–65). Hershey, PA: IGI Global; doi:10.4018/978-1-4666-4983-5.ch003

Swarnkar, M., & Bhadoria, R. S. (2016). Security Aspects in Utility Computing. In G. Deka, G. Siddesh, K. Srinivasa, & L. Patnaik (Eds.), *Emerging Research Surrounding Power Consumption and Performance Issues in Utility Computing* (pp. 262–275). Hershey, PA: IGI Global; doi:10.4018/978-1-4666-8853-7.ch012

Talamantes-Padilla, C. A., García-Alcaráz, J. L., Maldonado-Macías, A. A., Alor-Hernández, G., Sánchéz-Ramírez, C., & Hernández-Arellano, J. L. (2017). Information and Communication Technology Impact on Supply Chain Integration, Flexibility, and Performance. In M. Tavana, K. Szabat, & K. Puranam (Eds.), *Organizational Productivity and Performance Measurements Using Predictive Modeling and Analytics* (pp. 213–234). Hershey, PA: IGI Global; doi:10.4018/978-1-5225-0654-6.ch011

Tang, Z., & Pan, Y. (2015). Big Data Security Management. In N. Zaman, M. Seliaman, M. Hassan, & F. Marquez (Eds.), *Handbook of Research on Trends and Future Directions in Big Data and Web Intelligence* (pp. 53–66). Hershey, PA: IGI Global; doi:10.4018/978-1-4666-8505-5.ch003

Thakur, P. K., & Verma, A. (2015). Process Batch Offloading Method for Mobile-Cloud Computing Platform. [JCIT]. *Journal of Cases on Information Technology, 17*(3), 1–13. doi:10.4018/JCIT.2015070101

Thota, C., Manogaran, G., Lopez, D., & Vijayakumar, V. (2017). Big Data Security Framework for Distributed Cloud Data Centers. In M. Moore (Ed.), *Cybersecurity Breaches and Issues Surrounding Online Threat Protection* (pp. 288–310). Hershey, PA: IGI Global; doi:10.4018/978-1-5225-1941-6.ch012

Toor, G. S., & Ma, M. (2017). Security Issues of Communication Networks in Smart Grid. In M. Ferrag & A. Ahmim (Eds.), *Security Solutions and Applied Cryptography in Smart Grid Communications* (pp. 29–49). Hershey, PA: IGI Global; doi:10.4018/978-1-5225-1829-7.ch002

Wahi, A. K., Medury, Y., & Misra, R. K. (2015). Big Data: Enabler or Challenge for Enterprise 2.0. [IJSSMET]. *International Journal of Service Science, Management, Engineering, and Technology, 6*(2), 1–17. doi:10.4018/ijssmet.2015040101

Wang, H., Liu, W., & Soyata, T. (2014). Accessing Big Data in the Cloud Using Mobile Devices. In P. Raj & G. Deka (Eds.), *Handbook of Research on Cloud Infrastructures for Big Data Analytics* (pp. 444–470). Hershey, PA: IGI Global; doi:10.4018/978-1-4666-5864-6.ch018

Wang, M., & Kerr, D. (2017). Confidential Data Storage Systems for Wearable Platforms. In A. Marrington, D. Kerr, & J. Gammack (Eds.), *Managing Security Issues and the Hidden Dangers of Wearable Technologies* (pp. 74–97). Hershey, PA: IGI Global; doi:10.4018/978-1-5225-1016-1.ch004

Winter, J. S. (2015). Privacy Challenges for the Internet of Things. In M. Khosrow-Pour (Ed.), *Encyclopedia of Information Science and Technology* (3rd ed., pp. 4373–4383). Hershey, PA: IGI Global; doi:10.4018/978-1-4666-5888-2.ch429

Wolfe, M. (2017). Establishing Governance for Hybrid Cloud and the Internet of Things. In J. Chen, Y. Zhang, & R. Gottschalk (Eds.), *Handbook of Research on End-to-End Cloud Computing Architecture Design* (pp. 300–325). Hershey, PA: IGI Global; doi:10.4018/978-1-5225-0759-8.ch013

Yan, Z. (2014). Trust Management in Mobile Cloud Computing. In *Trust Management in Mobile Environments: Autonomic and Usable Models* (pp. 54–93). Hershey, PA: IGI Global; doi:10.4018/978-1-4666-4765-7.ch004

Zardari, M. A., & Jung, L. T. (2016). Classification of File Data Based on Confidentiality in Cloud Computing using K-NN Classifier. [IJBAN]. *International Journal of Business Analytics*, *3*(2), 61–78. doi:10.4018/IJBAN.2016040104

Zhang, C., Simon, J. C., & Lee, E. (2016). An Empirical Investigation of Decision Making in IT-Related Dilemmas: Impact of Positive and Negative Consequence Information. [JOEUC]. *Journal of Organizational and End User Computing*, *28*(4), 73–90. doi:10.4018/JOEUC.2016100105

About the Authors

Uri Shafrir is associate professor in Department of Human Development and Applied Psychology at Ontario Institute for Studies in Education and Director of Adult Study Skills Clinic at Faculty of Information of University of Toronto. His recent research focuses on concept parsing algorithms in various knowledge domains and on instructional methodologies for deep comprehension of conceptual content that enhance learning outcomes. Shafrir received doctorate in mathematical sciences from the University of California at Los Angeles and doctorate in developmental psychology from York University, Toronto. Shafrir was founder and director of the Institute of Planetary and Space Science at Tel-Aviv University; before moving to the University of Toronto he was Adjunct Professor at the University of Wisconsin and at Columbia University.

Masha Etkind is professor in the Department of Architectural Science at Ryerson University. She teaches design, theory and history of architecture. Her work and recent research focus on heritage conservation, language and roots of living architecture, as well as on Pedagogy for Conceptual Thinking in architectural education. Etkind received a professional degree in architecture from St. Petersburg University of Architecture and Engineering, and Masters in Architecture from the University of Toronto. Etkind is member of the Royal Architectural Institute of Canada.

Index

M

Meaning Equivalence (ME) 58-59, 64-65
Meaning Equivalence Reusable Learning Objects (MERLO) 80, 83, 89, 97, 103, 105
measurement 29, 104
MERLO Diagnostics of Misconceptions 84
metalanguage 7-8
multiple definitions of concepts 62, 64

N

natural language 7, 9, 25-26, 33-34, 104

P

Pedagogy for Conceptual Thinking 58, 66, 84, 86, 91, 93, 95, 97, 103
poor conceptual thinkers 92-95
post-failure reflectivity 13, 15
pre-failure reflectivity 15

R

representation 1-4, 7, 10-11, 14, 18-19, 31, 45-46, 59, 63, 92, 97, 107

representational competence 5-18, 80, 91

S

semantic search 69-70, 72
semiosphere 1, 8, 10, 17
semiotics 6, 8, 40
sign system 5-8, 17, 33, 60
Specific comprehension deficits 85
sublanguage 25, 30-32, 39-40, 42, 44, 58, 60, 64-65, 103-104, 108, 110, 112
super-ordinate concept 39-40, 42, 53, 58, 61, 63, 66, 70-71, 75, 78
Surface Similarity (SS) 64-65
symbolic environment 1, 8

T

Target Statement (TS) 58, 64-66, 81
text analysis 39, 105

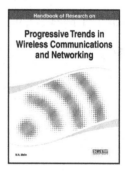

Become an IRMA Member

Members of the **Information Resources Management Association (IRMA)** understand the importance of community within their field of study. The Information Resources Management Association is an ideal venue through which professionals, students, and academicians can convene and share the latest industry innovations and scholarly research that is changing the field of information science and technology. Become a member today and enjoy the benefits of membership as well as the opportunity to collaborate and network with fellow experts in the field.

IRMA Membership Benefits:

- **One FREE Journal Subscription**

- **30% Off Additional Journal Subscriptions**

- **20% Off Book Purchases**

- Updates on the latest events and research on Information Resources Management through the IRMA-L listserv.

- Updates on new open access and downloadable content added to Research IRM.

- A copy of the Information Technology Management Newsletter twice a year.

- A certificate of membership.

IRMA Membership $195

Scan code or visit **irma-international.org** and begin by selecting your free journal subscription.

Membership is good for one full year.